D1511686

DATE			

TELEMANAGE YOUR CUSTOMERS
A SYSTEM FOR TELEPHONE ACCOUNT MANAGEMENT

Telemanage Your Customers

A system for telephone account management

Merlin Stone
Anna Thomson
Chris Wheeler

Gower

Published by
Gower Publishing Company Limited
Gower House
Croft Road
Aldershot
Hants GU11 3HR
England

Gower Publishing Company
Old Post Road
Brookfield
Vermont 05036
USA

British Library Cataloguing in Publication Data
Stone, Merlin *1948-*
    Telemanage your customers: a system for telephone account management.
    1. Companies. Financial management. Use of telephones
    I. Title II. Thomson, Anna III. Wheeler, Chris
    658.15

ISBN 0 566 02903 0

Printed and Bound by Woolnough Bookbinding, Irthlingborough, Northants.

Contents

Illustrations

Foreword

This book holds the key to managing your customers by telephone. In British Telecom, we call this "Telephone Account Management" (TAM). We use TAM to manage hundreds of thousands of customers because it is the best way to meet their needs.

Our business is a complex one. Many customers find it difficult to understand the mystique of communications technology. To help deal with this and respond to our customers' needs, we must provide trustworthy advice on what equipment and services to buy. Trust leads to sales, because "people buy from people they know". That is what our Telephone Account Managers are all about.

To us, the Telephone Account Manager is a sales person, with targets to achieve week-in, week-out. To our customers, the Telephone Account Manager is a personal sales consultant, who understands their business, advises and guides them as to what to buy, and then concludes the sale. All of this is done on the telephone.

TAM enables us to increase business with our customers in a planned but responsive way, at a lower cost and higher productivity that a traditional field sales force could achieve. It creates a firm but flexible discipline, which allows our people to move faster to capture opportunities and deal with problems.

Most important of all, in these competitive times, it ensures that we win against competitors. So, if you want to get closer to your customers and ensure that you are meeting their needs as completely and competitively as possible, I recommend that you read this book and then . . . act!

I wish you good luck in your venture and hope that your customers and your sales staff will soon be enjoying the full benefits of telephone account management.

Peter Macleod
Director, Worldwide Sales
British Telecom

Preface

The project on which we – the authors – came together was the British Telecom TAM project. In this project, the best American and British expertise was deployed to apply Telephone Account Management to one of British Telecom's most important market sectors. This was (and still is) one of the most advanced and largest marketing projects the UK has seen, affecting thousands of sales staff and millions of business customers.

British Telecom has an obvious and honest interest in helping more companies manage their customers using telecommunications. Anna led the team that made it work in British Telecom. Chris and Merlin helped in the training and documentation. We all feel that marketers need to understand how Telephone Account Management is implemented. We were privileged to be involved in the British Telecom project and hope this book does justice to it.

Merlin Stone
Anna Thomson
Chris Wheeler

May 1990

Acknowledgements

Our first debt is to British Telecom, which gave us the opportunity to work on the Telephone Account Management Project and, more specifically, allowed us to publish some aspects of our work. One of the British Telecom team leaders, Michael Tarte-Booth, deserves special mention. He led the implementation of the project. At the time of writing, he was still deeply involved in it. Otherwise, he would have had the time to be a co-author! Peter Macleod, British Telecom's Sales Director, has played a critical role in the continuing success of the project and in supporting the publication of this book.

Outside British Telecom, the biggest contributor by far to the methodology of Telephone Account Management, and therefore to the ideas which stimulated this book, was Rudi Oetting, one of America's leading telemarketing experts.

Finally, we should like to thank our families, who supported us while we wrote this book, an addition to already heavy workloads for all of us.

1

Is telemanaging for you?

Telemanaging customers is defined as follows:

> Managing the customer primarily through the medium of the telephone, using all the sales, marketing, systems and management disciplines of account management.

Telemanaging has its roots in the account management approach practised by companies selling into industrial markets. However there is a big difference between the normal field sales account manager and the telemanager. Account managers in field sales forces use the telephone mainly to fix appointments, trouble-shoot and follow-up the order process. But telemanagers use the telephone for all their contacts with customers. If a face-to-face call is required, the telemanager diaries it and makes arrangements for a specialist field salesperson to call. That field call is then followed up by the telemanager who remains responsible for the relationship with the customer.

'Telemanager' is short for the more accurate but cumbersome 'Telephone Account Manager'. The latter captures more fully the sense of account management. But to the uninitiated, it can sound like someone who makes sure you pay your telephone bills! Now that you have been introduced to the term, we shall start to use it. Fortunately, it lends itself to abbreviation, as TAM. When we use the expression 'the TAM', we are referring to the Telephone Account Manager — the person responsible for managing the customer over the telephone. 'TAM' by itself refers to the concept. Thus, the TAM 'telemanages' the customer, using telephone account management (TAM) disciplines and systems. To use TAM as a verb – to TAM – would be stretching things too far! So we use 'telemanage' for this. Finally, the term 'TAM manager' refers to someone who manages a team of TAMs. All this may sound rather dull. It fails to convey the excitement that we have felt in helping to make TAM happen. This involved implementing the combination of the best of marketing and sales practice with the best of telecommunications and computing technology. We know TAM works because we can point to it working. TAM is a leading edge concept. So far, it has only been deployed by companies which have:

- the foresight to see how TAM can solve at one stroke their problems of cost of sales and market coverage
- the competitive need to do it
- the resources, energy and commitment to make it happen
- the willingness to take the risks involved

Many more companies are, however,

1

considering TAM. They will need to understand how TAM works, why it works, and what are the resource implications of TAM. That is why we have written this book.

How different is TAM?

Is TAM really such an innovation? If all it does is to combine good account management with the telephone, does it really need a whole book? The difference between TAM and normal management may not sound very great. But the difference is greatly magnified when we start to examine why and how telephone account management is used. For a TAM typically manages many more customers than the account manager, sometimes ten or even a hundred times as many. To do this well, the TAM must be supported properly by computer and telecommunications systems, support staff, management and even furniture. Those responsible for managing TAM in, and keeping TAM going, must get their staff to combine account management and telemarketing skills — a difficult combination. The managers themselves must have the political and management skills to:

- introduce TAM into the organization
- integrate it with all other distribution and marketing communication policies, structures and initiatives
- keep it on track
- ensure that it yields the maximum commercial benefits to their company

The cost/coverage trap

One reason why TAM is becoming such a popular approach to managing customers is that more and more companies are being caught in the cost/coverage trap. The costs of keeping a sales person in the field are rising. This forces many companies into premature moves to cut their sales force and use indirect channels of distribution. But at the same time, the desirability of the account management approach to selling is increasing. Markets are becoming more competitive. Buyers are becoming more professional. They expect better levels of service from companies who want their business. Turning them over to a dealer or distributor has to be done very carefully. It can compromise the quality of service the customer receives. Worse, it may open the door to competition, sometimes even through the same dealer. In this situation, some companies realize the need to evaluate how they manage their customers. They rightly start with an analysis of their customer base. This might show the classic 80:20 situation, or something similar: 80 per cent of their revenue (and a higher proportion of their profit) comes from 20 per cent of their customers. Figure 1.1 depicts what this analysis might show when the customer base is split into deciles by a company's sales to them.

By itself, the chart in Figure 1.1 might be misleading. It is not just the revenue coming from each customer that determines customer profitability. Average order size is also important. This is particularly so if your industry is one where marketing and selling costs take a high proportion of revenue, for example, computers, life assurance. In this case, marketing costs are likely to be affected by the way in which sales are achieved and orders are placed. If your product has a complex sales cycle, then a customer who places many small orders will be more expensive to serve than one who places one large order. So average order size will be important. Here again, the 80:20 rule is likely to apply, as in Figure 1.2. If there is a neat match between high revenue customers and high average order value customers, well and good. You can match a high cost sales channel to those customers, to

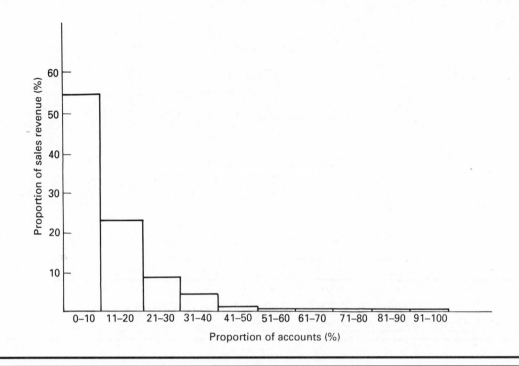

Figure 1.1 Distribution of account size

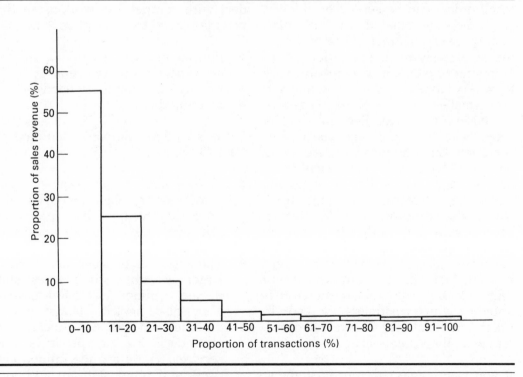

Figure 1.2 Distribution of transaction size

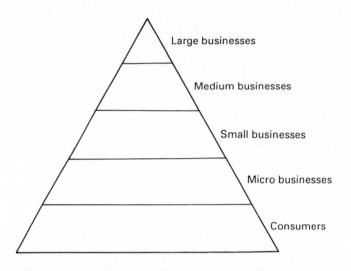

Figure 1.3 Distribution of customer size

serve them well and defend them against competition. Meanwhile, customers who order less and who place small orders can be served by a lower cost, more automated but still high quality sales channel. However, the match is rarely neat. The order size of your larger customers will probably vary from very large to very small, while even your smallest customers may occasionally place a large order. Remember, at no stage have we mentioned *potential* or company size. The measurement so far has been by size of your customers' orders from you! If you do the same exercise by customer size (e.g. turnover), the problem will be worse, because your share of their business will vary. What seems to you to be a small customer, placing a small order every now and then, may turn out to have very high potential. The problem therefore is knowing which customers are ready to order, and what they are likely to order, and what their potential is.

If you have neglected your customers, you may also be faced with the problem of competition hitting your customer base. They will look for your soft underbelly, and find it with your smaller customers or your marginal accounts (companies who buy little from you). To deal with competition working in this way, you need to be very active in:

- finding out where and when you *don't* meet customer needs
- finding out what these needs are
- meeting them

In this situation, companies tend to find the following:

- Their largest customers (key accounts) are well managed and properly developed by experienced sales staff talking to key decision-makers, *but. . .*
- The pressures of work mean that in larger accounts, their sales staff neglect minor decision-makers. They also neglect people whose attitudes and activities affect important decisions on products and services. These include influencers, users and other staff. In addition, non-routine, new applications springing from new users within these accounts might be missed. As

these new applications replace older ones, the company might eventually be branded as old-fashioned and unresponsive to customer needs, and be excluded from new applications.

- Medium-sized customers are contacted proactively and reasonably often by territorial sales staff. But the way in which they are managed is not comprehensive enough to ensure that the business potential is maximized and the competitive threat minimized.
- Smaller customers — the bottom layers — are communicated with when they place an order, experience a problem or ask for information. They are covered by advertisements in the trade press or elsewhere. The occasional mail shot is sent to them; if they are lucky perhaps a catalogue. If they are fortunate, they might receive the occasional telephone call or sales visit to persuade them to buy a specific product, their need for which has not been established.

The situation is summarized in Figure 1.3. This analysis leads most companies to conclude that their need for more regular, in-depth and proactive contact affects all sizes of customer. They might boost the support given to managers of larger customers, but they face a problem with smaller customers, given the costs of field sales staff.

Ten years ago, there were few options. One option was to ask the calling sales force to increase its productivity. At worst, this meant fewer, shorter calls. Only the best companies analysed the working practices of their sales forces. This might show that field sales staff were spending too much time on administration and trouble-shooting, too little time on customer work. Simplification of administration and clear division of roles between selling and support would often be the chosen

policy. Yet even companies which went through with this discovered that cost pressures caught up with them. The other option was that the customer had to be served by a third party. The customer who suffered most from these developments was usually the middle-order customer, who was not large enough to merit the account manager, but was too large to be satisfied with the kind of service provided by the distributor. Middle-order customers wanted to be handled directly by the original supplier, but were given the choice between rare calls from a field sales person, or being referred to a dealer.

The TAM option

Today, all that has changed. As companies scrutinize the cost-effectiveness of their marketing channels, more and more are turning to TAM. They see it as the prime channel for certain purposes, such as:

- managing smaller customers, whose usual purchasing frequency and/or value is too low to justify a calling sales force
- managing specific aspects of larger customers' needs (e.g. additional products, add-ons, peripherals, supplies, services, support, etc.)
- carrying out needs-identification work over a sustained period, and developing sales over time at an affordable cost

In some cases, TAM is being used with a calling sales force, with the sales force working to TAM disciplines. This is particularly effective with products and services which are:

- technically very complex
- require a high degree of custom-

ization to customer needs
- information-intense (e.g. complex life insurance and investment packages)

Controlling sales costs

One of the most important financial benefits of TAM is that the cost of selling is under much tighter control than in the traditional field sales force. It is not a cheap channel, but its costs can be controlled more tightly to ensure that profitability on each customer account remains at the right level. For example, a customer who is loyal but with low revenue potential can simply have calls diaried less frequently, while contact is sustained by mail. At the other extreme, a high potential customer can be called more frequently, with field sales staff working under TAM disciplines. An important additional benefit is that the *spread* of costs can be reduced. Individual TAM productivity can be very closely monitored and the content of conversations with customers can be redirected by management so as to improve productivity.

Thus, sales costs can be tuned to stay within the marketing margin available per transaction. 'Marketing margin' is the sum available after all non-marketing costs and target profit have been deducted from revenue. The marketing margin per transaction is best measured in cash rather than percentage terms. This is because cash tells you how much you can afford to spend on marketing to secure the transaction. The cash marketing margin available in a big transaction (whether it consists of one large item or many small ones) is normally larger than that available in smaller transactions.

How this affects customer-base management is shown in Figure 1.4. The 80:20 effect appears when transactions are represented by available marketing margin. The ideal sales channel mix varies from the calling sales force at one end, to catalogues and retail outlets or dealerships at the other. Also shown is how important it is not to stick rigidly to only one sales channel for a given customer. Telemanaging customers

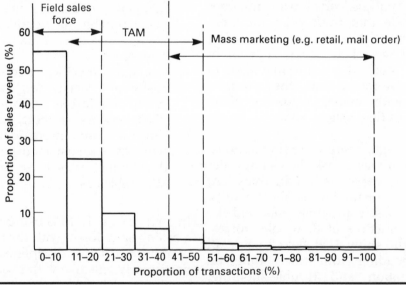

Figure 1.4 Matching sales channels to transactions

allows the relatively low-cost telephone relationship to be the means by which the sales channel relationship is customized to every transaction. One day a customer may discuss with the TAM when the field salesperson should call; the next day, the customer may place orders with the TAM from the catalogue. Demonstration or retail channels may also be used by the TAM to promote a sale, while casual 'walk-in' visits from customers can be followed up by the TAM. This approach also allows the *outbound* (from you to your customer) and the *inbound* (from your customer to you) relationships to work smoothly together, because they are focused in one person — the TAM. That is, instead of asking your customer to face a myriad of possible ways of dealing with you, you offer them a smoothly co-ordinated route. You can only do this because you have decided to invest in the TAM concept, and support it with the right campaigns, procedures and systems — for managing the customer and for managing your company to manage the customer! You also need the right internal communications approach, to make sure that the people responsible for the customer talk to each other.

Additional benefits

Once a company has taken up the TAM approach, it realizes that there are other advantages. Marketing and sales campaigns can be mounted more quickly relative to other channels of communication. The customer begins to feel that the company is more responsive. Orders and enquiries are dealt with on the spot, instead of waiting for an exchange of letters. The small customer who receives a mailshot two or three times a year really appreciates the difference, and now gets called four or five times a year. At each call, the customer is asked pertinent questions, has personal queries resolved, and can place an order without any fuss. Instead of waiting for the customer to contact a competitor, or

worse, for a competitor to contact the customer, the company using TAM keeps the situation under control and keeps the customer happy.

Companies taking up the TAM approach can find another benefit. They may be spending much on advertising and direct mail, but not moving close enough to customers who receive these communications. Entering into a proper telemanaged dialogue means that the power of advertising and direct mail can be converted more quickly into orders. For this to happen, however, the work of the TAMs and of these other means of marketing communication must be properly co-ordinated. This requires not only alignment of policy, but also investment in proper marketing databases.

A further benefit of TAM is that tighter management control of selling is achieved. A TAM operation produces a flow of statistics about how customers are behaving. This contrasts with the classic problem faced by sales managers — obtaining enough information from their field sales staff without turning them into market researchers. This benefit is particularly important for companies facing increased competition in established markets. Here, sales force management disciplines might not be strong enough to withstand competitive pressures. If sales management needs more information about which customers are buying, when and why, the TAM operation can provide it.

Finally, a company whose products are innovative, requiring some explanation and subsequent nurturing of customers, needs to stay in close contact with its customers and prospects. It may want to husband its resources to deal directly only with its large customers. Neglecting its smaller customers just at the moment when its product should be sold equally hard to them is an invitation to competitors. Telemanaging is a good way to stop this.

Telemanaging in consumer markets

Much of the experience with TAM has been in industrial markets. Consumer markets which have a high enough average frequency of purchase and large enough average transaction size to justify the frequency of contact involved in TAM are fewer. However, there are some. Examples include the marketing of financial products to high-net-worth individuals, the marketing of automobile products (vehicles, service, rental) to multi-vehicle families, and the marketing of holiday products to frequent-holiday families.

Many very small (one-person or single family) businesses are hybrids. They are both consumer and industrial customers. For such businesses, decisions on the above products may be taken on a mixture of business and personal criteria. So while telemanaging may not be appropriate for the average consumer, it may be just right for such businesses.

Does TAM save money?

There is one area where companies sometimes look for an advantage in TAM and are disappointed because it has not been achieved – TAM is sometimes seen as a way of reducing marketing costs as a proportion of revenue. In most industries, there is a surprising constancy in the costs of getting a product or service to the customer, and even radically different marketing methods show surprisingly similar proportionate marketing costs. For example, the costs of marketing clothes via mail order or through a high street store are about the same. But the benefits of doing it through both channels is the increased *market coverage*. If a company uses both approaches, it

participates in more buying decisions – many of which it has stimulated. In some cases, using TAM is the only way of *staying* in some markets, particularly if product prices are falling there, TAM may allow you to reduce marketing costs as a proportion of revenue. However, mostly it will provide a way of maintaining or increasing market coverage while holding marketing costs at their current percentage of revenue.

The role of technology

What is increasingly allowing more companies to use TAM in many different ways is the development of computer and telecommunications technology. The database marketing approach has arrived. Companies are investing in the most important prerequisite of TAM – a database of all customers and contacts. This is combined with the right telecommunications technology and mini- or microcomputer systems for managing the daily activities of the TAM operation, to produce the support the TAM needs.

Direct marketing's role

Going into database marketing implies an acceptance of direct marketing, another important discipline for TAM. Direct marketing involves creating a dialogue with customers using a variety of contact media. These include media advertising, telephone, mail, exhibitions, seminars, showrooms, and the sales force. These are combined into a campaign consisting of a series of contacts which are well targeted and timed. Through these campaigns, customers are exposed to offers which are expressed in terms of benefits to them.

Telemarketing and TAM

The fastest growing direct marketing medium is telemarketing. Telemarketing, a related discipline, should not be confused with telemanaging. Many companies are starting to truly telemanage their customers, from developing initial contacts right through to closing the sale and developing long-term relationships such that the individual sales cycles merge into each other.

Telemarketing is often used as a support to other sales channels, and is sometimes used to carry out tasks which the principal channel cannot carry out cost-effectively. For example, in some businesses, a direct sales force is a relatively expensive tool to use for identifying and qualifying customers. So telemarketing, perhaps combined with other marketing approaches (e.g direct mail), is used to identify and qualify customers. TAM, however, is a specific application of telemarketing and a fully fledged sales and account management channel in its own right, and combines telemarketing disciplines with the those of direct and database marketing and of account management. Choosing TAM strategically involves commitment to a new sales channel – a highly efficient form of account management.

TAM and account management

TAM cannot work well if your company is not committed to the account management approach. We shall examine the main elements of the approach later (see Chapter 4). TAM, however, is *not* for you if your company is not committed to:

- developing a long-term dialogue with its customers
- developing a relationship with its customers that works not just at the commercial level, but also at the personal acquaintance level
- investing in customers so that they buy from you over the long term

TAM is a high-volume, telephone-based operation. But it aims to follow all the rules of good account management, so that customers are cared for and their needs met. The concept of 'flogging widgets or boxes' to customers, of 'shifting tin or plastic', because the warehouse is full, is utterly alien to the TAM concept and its *modus operandi*.

How long does it take?

Introducing telemanagement can take a long time. From the time your marketing and sales management is faced with a blank piece of paper headed 'Business Plan', to the time when you have a team of TAMs installed in their room, happily calling customers, could be between six months and a year. From the day that the TAM operation goes live to the point where TAMs have built a position of personal trust and understanding with customers that is generating major sales may take longer again – up to another year, and depends on:

- the nature of the customer's previous relationship with your company (in terms of personal relationships and sales orders)
- the frequency of the TAM contact

Having developed a 'model' of how TAM should be implemented in a single office, and used project management software to check that this model is totally consistent and does not stretch resources unduly, we can advise you to consider the same idea yourself. More details are given later (see Chapter 7). If you use this approach, you can develop a coherent plan of action and diary dates when you need to start and finish tasks to ensure that your 'go live' date is achieved. You can view your project in many different ways, but most importantly, TAM enables you to arrange diaried events, and to identify changes necessitated as a result of any errors.

Now all you need to do is to understand in more detail what TAM is, what it does, and how to set it up – in other words, read on!

2

How telemanaging works

TAMs are responsible for their own accounts. The TAM is the person that every member of the customer's staff who needs help in buying your products should call. The TAM calls key staff (buyers, principal users, influencers) several times a year. During each call, the TAM:

- updates your company's knowledge of the customer's situation and needs
- checks whether any problems need solving
- advises on products and services
- takes orders
- diaries the next call

TAMs are not generalists, but trained sales people. They handle a wide portfolio of your company's products and services, carefully chosen to match the needs of their target market. They are targeted to achieve high revenue. But like all account managers, they are also consultants. They help the customer deal with problems, particularly those related to obtaining service from your company. However, supporting TAMs with a filter for inbound service calls may improve customer handling and maintain a high level of TAM productivity.

Face-to-face contact

How face-to-face contact fits in

Where field sales staff work with TAMs, they do so as part of a team, not as independent sales staff who occasionally make a call booked by a TAM – this would be a recipe for disaster. The field salesperson works in harmony with the TAM, making face-to-face calls while the TAM is managing the account on the telephone. Face-to-face contact with customers may be needed when a demonstration or in-depth needs analysis is required. The TAM and the field salesperson work as a team to maximize joint commission, so the commission plan must be carefully designed to reflect and encourage their joint efforts. Together, the TAM and the field salesperson maximize coverage of the customer base, with each playing their own important part.

Criteria for the face-to-face call

To ensure cost-effective involvement of field sales-staff, clear criteria must be set for their involvement. These include:

- the need to ensure customer satisfaction
- likely order size

- complexity of product or service under discussion
- uncertainty about the kind of product or service that will meet the customer's need
- whether the customer strongly requests a visit

The last point may seem a little strange. Surely, when a customer requests the salesperson to call, the call should be made? However, meeting customer needs does not mean doing everything the customer asks. TAMs must be trained to first find out whether such a call will really add value.

Starting the telemanaging relationship

At the start of the TAM's relationship with the customer, the TAM introduces the service and reinforces the two-way communication. Time is spent gathering information from the customer. The TAM develops a clear understanding of:

- what the customer's objectives and strategies are
- how your company's products can help the customer achieve them
- who are the important contacts in the customer's organization
- how the customer currently uses your (and competitors') products and services

Only when this knowledge base has been built is the TAM in a position to advise the customer.

From the customer's point of view, the TAM is introduced as a new point of contact, and the only or dominant point of *sales* contact. The TAM is responsible to customers for ensuring that your company meets their needs. If a customer is new, or has been neglected for a long time, there is no single right

sales approach for the first call. The TAM uses the information you have about the customer to decide what is the appropriate course of action. The best starting point is to ask customers some questions about their past needs and how they have been met. However, as soon as the customer is ready, the TAM moves the customer into a structured relationship.

Structured selling

TAM selling is a structured process. It starts with needs analysis to identify customer requirements. To ensure that the correct questions are asked and the right products and services offered, TAMs are provided with call guides. These are very important at the beginning of the relationship. At this stage, matters may be sensitive. The TAM's skills may be new and untested, so call objectives for the early stages of a TAM operation are limited.

Relationship selling

As the relationship develops, the TAM can develop a fully consultative relationship with the customer. The objective is that the customer develops trust in your company through the TAM. The customer begins to accord the TAM the role of consultant in allowing him to propose solutions to business problems. Like any good consultant, the TAM collects the appropriate information through structured questioning to identify customer needs. The questioning also provides information for estimating the business likely to result from satisfaction of these needs. To fulfil the consultative role, the TAM must also know his or her own company's products and services well enough to offer the right option and the right solutions.

Meanwhile, the TAM keeps in touch

with the customer's basic needs and ensures that they are met. When TAMs succeed in developing this relationship, they can start to develop the market much more effectively, but always in a controlled and measured way. The direct marketing disciplines of productivity, measurement and testing are always present. We aim to get the TAM selling as much as possible as early as possible, by finding out what works and making sure it is used.

As with all account management, a structured approach is needed. If the TAM departs from this structure, it should only be because he knows the customer well enough and believes he can manage the account more productively using a less formal approach.

The call

The customer call is the focal point for the contact cycle. During the course of each call, the TAM takes orders. At the end of each call, the TAM establishes when the next contact should be and diaries it. Confirmation of the order, including delivery arrangements where possible, is sent to the customer.

After the call, any additional information requested is also sent. The information may be sent directly from the TAM office. In larger companies, a request may be logged on the marketing database, so that a fulfilment house sends the information. Finally, any information collected is communicated to the customer database (this may have occurred automatically through scripted questions). If the customer requires face-to-face contact, either by a sales force call or by a visit to a showroom, these are diaried.

How often should you call?

The number of calls a TAM needs to make to a given customer to achieve the kind of relationship described above depends upon

- the size of customer
- the type of product
- the volume, frequency and complexity of need
- the customer's own preference for frequency of call

For example, a small business customer for computer supplies might warrant a call once every two months, but a large customer for the same products might require a call every week.

Results

If all this is done, what results will you get? Experience suggests that if you take the proper account management approach, and avoid trying to sell hard on the first call, the following will result:

- Your customers will welcome TAM. They will want to be dealt with more positively, personally and helpfully.
- They will make commitments by phone.
- They will order more frequently.
- They will order more products during one call.
- They will order a wider range of products, often including ones which were not the subject of the call.
- They are more likely to go through with orders (i.e. not to cancel).
- Field sales staff closing TAM-stimulated calls will have higher closing rates.
- Learning more about customer needs (which should be allowed for in sales targets which are initially lower) will allow you to achieve higher revenue and profit.
- You will have more control over every aspect of the sales cycle and of the account development process than with any other sales channel.

The need for integration

Experience has highlighted the need for the approach to customers to be as integrated as possible. The systems need to be integrated, to minimize the use of paper. Processes need to be integrated, so that the customer sees a natural relationship between the role of the TAM and other contact staff (e.g. field sales, customer service). Most important of all, however, is that the entire marketing process, from strategic marketing planning through to implementation 'on the ground', should work in an integrated way, such that:

- the responsibility for handling every customer is clearly allocated
- the customer perceives that every aspect of his relationship with your company is being professionally managed

Marketing the relationship to the customer

We have already emphasized that the TAM relationship should not be adopted just for reasons of cost-effectiveness. The research shows that it gives better sales service to customers. To ensure that the customer obtains the full benefit from the relationship, you must market it to them.

On the first call, therefore, the TAM must explain the nature of the relationship. The relationship must be carefully positioned, as adding to – rather than detracting from – what the customer is currently receiving in terms of marketing attention. Remember, in many cases the customer is receiving very little, and usually much less than marketing management thinks! It is important that this marketing 'positioning' of the TAM

is supported in the field by calling sales staff. This is yet another reason why the relationship between the TAM and field staff should be absolutely clear. Otherwise, conflict between the two could occur, and would be very damaging to both sides.

Combining the disciplines of direct and database marketing, telemarketing and account management, to produce the kind of cost-effective and customer-oriented marketing described above, is not easy. It demands:

- careful planning and implementation
- integration with the overall marketing approach of the company

Many companies, stimulated by the cost and competitive pressures mentioned above, turn to TAM too hastily. As a result, they get their fingers burnt because they were not aware of the costs of implementing TAM properly, or because they implemented it badly and failed to achieve the desired results. When it comes to quality, telemanaging does not tolerate compromises. You must not compromise on your objectives or on quality. In our experience, to achieve a professional TAM operation, you must persevere to attain your objectives. If you compromise on what you need, you're likely to compromise results.

Who should use TAM?

Our aim is to show you how to develop and implement TAM properly, based upon experience of working with companies who are using the TAM approach. Naturally, companies who might want to use TAM come in all shapes and sizes. Existing and potential users of TAM include suppliers of:

- industrial equipment and services
- office equipment, computer and telecommunications systems, equipment and supplies
- management services
- financial services
- business travel services

Companies using TAM range from the smallest company, serving a local or regional market from a single office, possibly with only two or three TAMs calling, to the largest national or multinational company, with several TAM offices, spread over one or more countries.

TAM – assumptions

TAM is designed to meet all needs. The needs only differ in scale. To work, TAM involves a high degree of personal contact between the TAM and customers, i.e. two-way personalized communication. Telemanaging does not imply massive offices filled with hundreds of TAMs calling customers they have never heard of or seen. This is clearly not account management, but it may be very good telemarketing under some conditions. However, we have made a number of concessions to the larger company, as follows:

1 We assume that the TAM operation draws its information from a wider company marketing database of customers. If this does not exist already, then it can be developed using standard direct and telemarketing software packages available from many suppliers, to organize data from existing sales records.

2 We assume that the company has an established direct marketing operation. This should have an efficient mechanism for getting information to customers (e.g. brochures), via a request logged on the customer database, which is then transmitted to the mailing organization (often an external mailing or fulfilment house).

To meet the needs of smaller companies, and to large companies who want assurance before automating the computing and telecommunications systems, TAM can be run using paper-based forms and reports. This involves using microcomputers for the word processing and simple reporting that is found in almost every office today, however small. Of course, TAM can be run fully automated also.

The difference between the automated and non-automated approach is very small. The automated approach is easier to run (there is less paper), but implies a greater initial investment. If the TAM operation is very busy (as it should be), however, paper can accumulate very quickly. You will also find it difficult to maintain staff. In a big company, a paper-based approach runs a real risk of confusing the customer, because there is no way of keeping all the right systems and people informed of the results of calls which are recorded only on paper.

Before we show how to implement TAM, we need to describe the marketing context within which TAM operates, as this affects many of the procedures used in TAM.

3

The marketing background

The benefits of TAM stem directly from the fact that telemanaging combines a number of best-practice marketing techniques into a single approach to managing customers. If you are to run your TAM operation smoothly and effectively, you must understand these techniques. You must be sure that TAM is right for your company. The reasons that underlie your entry into TAM will determine *how* you should implement and use TAM. For example, you may be using TAM to penetrate more deeply into your markets within large customer accounts (e.g. to manage a large number of decision-makers, influencers, and so on). If so, the nature of your relationship with customers (e.g. type, frequency and outcomes of calls) will be very different from where you use TAM to manage large numbers of small customers. The topics pertinent to this are:

- Customer orientation in marketing
- Account management
- Selling
- Channels of distribution and communications
- Database marketing
- The campaign process
- Branding
- Telemarketing

Customer orientation in marketing

Marketing can be made to seem very complicated, but its biggest successes come from following a few key principles, and implementing them thoroughly. If you do this, you will gain more customers and create better relationships with your existing customers.

Having a better relationship with customers means you can obtain more information about them. For example, salespeople who know their way around an account also know how to get even more information about it. The better you know your customers, the more you can satisfy their needs. In other words, the better you are at marketing, the more you learn about your customers. The more you learn about them, the better you get at marketing to them! The effectiveness of TAM *depends* on this principle. We call it 'the virtuous circle'.

The key to good marketing is 'customer orientation'. This does *not* mean giving the customer everything! It *does* mean striving to identify customer needs and meeting them – profitably. It also means working out what the different elements

17

of your customer management are, and what they are costing you, so that you can concentrate on managing your relationship with the customer more cost-effectively while improving the relationship. Customer orientation is not just an attitude of mind – it is a complete way of doing business.

The principles of customer orientation are:

- Customers are your greatest asset. Without them your business would die. Building and conserving this asset is the central task of marketing (and of TAM!). To do this,
- You must understand your customers' needs better than your competitors. You must use this understanding to meet these needs better than your competitors do. For some customers, TAM will be the main channel through which information about their needs is gathered, and through which their needs are satisfied.
- You will be able to understand and meet your customers' needs if you put them first. This means managing your day-to-day work to deliver the best results to customers. Customers do not belong to you by right, but by your hard, customer-oriented work. TAM is designed with the customer in mind. It aims to make the customer feel that he is being well-managed by you, while you meet your business objectives. A well-managed customer is more satisfied, orders more, and stays with you longer.

Lack of customer orientation is a common problem. Many companies are inward-looking. They are concerned with solving their own problems of product design, production or sales, or – worse – with their internal politics. They forget the needs of their customers. If their market becomes more competitive, they need to change to a more customer-oriented approach. This

requires the following changes:

- Their business policy must be founded on customer needs rather than just their own needs.
- They must identify these customer needs before designing products, rather than after.
- They should determine administrative procedures according to customers' requirements rather than internal convenience.
- They must listen to customers before promoting products to them.
- They should promote products in terms of the benefits of these products to customers, rather than the features which have been built into them.
- They must measure success in terms of satisfaction indices or responses to direct marketing campaigns, as well as sales.

In these circumstances, telemanaging comes into its own. The whole concept is based on customers' need to be managed well. Surveys and experience show how appreciative customers are when this happens. But do not despair if you do not recognize your company in the above ideal. You can break bad habits by learning from what your customers tell their TAMs.

As a company becomes more customer-oriented, it starts to use various measures of its success in meeting customer needs. Sales levels remain important, but other measures begin to be used. These include customer satisfaction and the extent to which customers 'feel' they are account-managed. These measures can be transformed into targets for marketing managers. These are needed because increased customer orientation cannot be achieved without increasing *accountability* for it. As we shall see, TAM has its own measures. Many of these have their roots in the well-established idea of account management.

How can a customer tell when a company is customer-oriented?

The main factors we look for in determining the strength of a company's customer orientation are as follows:

- When the company's products meet customer needs. They may even be slightly ahead of customers' immediate requirements, but customers rapidly 'latch on' to them because the products open up new areas of possible satisfaction.
- When products and services required by customers are in stock or can be installed when the customer wants.
- When customers' requests for information are answered accurately and promptly.
- When customers' problems are solved promptly.
- When communications from the company seem appropriate, relevant and intelligible.
- When contact with the company leaves the customer feeling more satisfied than before the contact.
- When customers recommend the company to others with similar needs.
- When the customer base continues to grow almost without loss of customers. New customers are attracted partly by the company's reputation for handling existing customers.

Account management

When a company is young and growing fast, its main aim is usually just to increase its customer base as fast as possible. If it has a direct sales force, it aims to get sales staff to identify as many good prospects as possible. Prospecting

– finding new customers – is the focus of sales activity.

As a company grows, it reaches a situation where most of its business comes from customers who have already bought from it or are using its services. The number of products and services offered by the company may increase, to meet customer needs. Managing customers becomes a complex business. They have many needs, and the company has many products to meet them. The responsibility for buying, recommending or using products may be spread very widely in the customer organization.

Competitors will complicate the situation. Companies then often appoint account managers to look after some of their customers. Their role differs between customers. If your company has account managers, their job description might include the following elements.

- Manage the commercial dialogue with the customer and resulting transactions.
- Act as the main interface between your company and the customer. In many companies, the account manager has principal responsibility for the sales interface, but may work with other sales staff (e.g. specialists). The account manager may also have general responsibility for service, support, customer administration (e.g. invoices) and any other function that comes into direct contact with the customer.
- Identify all relevant customer needs (now and in the future). This covers which products and services are needed, what they are used for, and the benefits that are obtained from using them.
- Understand the business situation and organization of the customer, and how they influence the customer's need for products and

services, and ability to pay for them!

- Understand the process by which the customer decides to buy relevant products and services (budgeting, decision-making, etc.)
- Become part of the process and act as a consultant to the customer. This includes helping them deal with problems and capture new opportunities through using your company's products and services.
- Present the benefits for the customer of doing business with you.
- Identify competitive threats to your position within the account.
- Provide information about the customer to the rest of your company.
- Provide the customer with information and with a channel for influencing your company.

All the above points should be geared to maximize customer sales and profitability.

The account manager must be the supplier's representative to the customer, and the customer's representative to the supplier. A good account management system has the effect of tying the customer and supplier closely together. It does this by ensuring that both derive great benefit from their relationship.

The depth of the relationship varies with the following:

- *The type of product or service.* The more important the product or service is to the customer's own business, the greater the potential for a close relationship, and the greater the desire of the customer for such a relationship.
- *The level of potential business in each customer.* If it is very small, then the supplier may find it uneconomic to invest in developing a close relationship. However, by using TAM, and carefully planning the call frequency, a company can extend the

principle of account management a long way down the market.

- *The range of needs that have to be covered.* Simple needs met by a few products and services do not require deep relationships. Complex needs and great product and service variety do!

From the customer's point of view, the TAM *is* your company. The TAM is the sales channel through which the customer is addressed, and a focal point for communication in both directions.

Technically complex products

If you have a product which is technically very complex or with high information content, you need to be careful how much of the customer service role of the account manager you allocate to the TAM. The job of the TAM must be primarily to sell, otherwise you will face real problems in justifying the investment. The TAM must not be a pigeon-hole for all customer queries. Many companies which merged the roles of the selling account manager and the query-resolving account manager discovered that this damaged sales productivity.

We recommend you separate the two account management roles. Make your TAMs account managers who sell. Give the customer service role (account administration and query handling) to another unit, working closely with the TAMs. The TAM's role is primarily one of attacking competition by getting to sales opportunities first and closing them, not defending by giving good after-sales service. The more the TAM succeeds in selling the right products to customers, the closer the bond between your company and your customers and the better your defence against competition. In technical telemarketing terms, if your TAMs spend most of their time dealing with inbound queries, they will be unable to create a timed, structured sales dialogue with customers.

The account managing 'type'

Many types of people succeed in account management. Some are aggressive individuals, who command customers' respect through the ability to manage complex sales and implement projects authoritatively. Some are the 'softly-softly' type, strong on listening skills and expert at getting customers to devise their own solutions – using their company's products and services. But not all customers expect the same approach. Nor do all users of the account management approach require the same style. If anything is certain, it is that the outstanding account manager deploys many skills differently according to the type of customer and type of selling task.

What sort of abilities and skills does he need? Here is a list of those generally felt to be necessary:

- Skills of questioning and listening, so as to build up a picture of the customer's needs. So are skills of sorting out relevant information. The ability to visualize the customer's premises, operational area and actual problems is crucial when working solely on the telephone.
- Analytical skills – the ability to make sense of customer information, and to put it together with information about company products and services to identify opportunities.
- Product knowledge – not necessarily in technical terms, but in terms that make sense to the customer.
- The ability to express what the company offers (its products, support, commitment, etc) in terms of benefits to customers, not just features and functions. Benefits express how a product meets a customer's needs, in the language

the customer has used to define these needs. We have to answer the question the customer asks – 'what will it do for me?'
- The ability to devise relevant options, so that the customer considers there is a real choice, and to match them to different benefits.
- Negotiating and influencing skills – knowing how to win people's hearts and minds, when to give and when to take, and the ability to handle problems and objections.
- A steady and strong activity rate, combined with diligence and determination. This does not necessarily mean calling a multitude of customers, as they may not be good prospects. It does mean working hard and preparing thoroughly, so that every call is an effective one. It also means maintaining a frequency of contact with the customer that the customer perceives to be right. It means determining call objectives and pursing them thoroughly. However, the smaller the customers, and the lower their average potential, the higher the calling rate required.
- Self-management skills – presentation, time management, organization of information, etc.
- Consultative skills. These include the ability to see things from the customers' point of view, to identify tasks that need to be done, to recommend how they should be done, and how to use your products and services to ensure that they will be done. This is 'solution selling'. It forms a particularly important part of account defence. Consultative skills are used to show customers how their business problems can be solved by your products and services. The promotional material your customers receive should focus on benefits, not features, and provide TAMs with keys to improve their consultative selling performance.
- The ability to foresee problems that

21

might arise, before or after the sale, and neutralize them.
- The ability to handle rejection positively.

The TAM's job is part of the evolution of the 'great tradition' of account management. But TAM is a very different proposition from, say, major account management. Both require account management skills, but the pace and focus of activity is different. Major account management is rather like the traditional, hand-crafted approach. TAM is the high-technology factory. Therefore, TAMs must be time-effective. They must acquire additional skills in managing customers time-effectively and remotely. They must learn to work with the systems that have been developed to allow them to do this. It is the combination of account management disciplines, activity rate disciplines and dedicated computer systems that makes the TAM concept so effective. But it is the quality of first-line TAM management that determines the quality and productivity of TAMs and hence their level of success.

Selling

What is selling? It is an integral part of marketing. Marketing is defined as how we identify customer needs and find ways to meet them profitably. Selling is defined as how we:

- target individual customers
- identify their needs
- motivate them to buy standard or customized versions of products and services that we have designed to meet the needs of the market of which they are part

Marketing cannot succeed without selling, and selling has a hard time without marketing!

The sales process is usually described as a multi-stage process. The simplest model is a three-stage one, as follows:

Identifying suspects

Finding out which people or businesses seem most likely to want your products and services. If you do not identify prospects, your market coverage is weak, and you open the door to competition. However mature your company's market, you may still need to identify opportunities to turn your customers into customers for your newer products.

Identifying prospects

By qualifying suspects according to factors such as the intensity of their need, timing of likely purchase, presence of competitive threat, availability of budget, and so on.

Turning prospects into customers

By proposing products and services to them in a form which meets their needs, by giving them real options from which to choose, by negotiating, handling objections and closing the sale, and by managing the process after the sale. These are the real 'sharp-end' sales skills, possession of which quickly sorts out the wheat from the chaff.

An account manager usually has a defined group of customers, but he still has to identify which of them are good prospects – even account managers have to go through the full sales cycle. They may not have to do all this job themselves. Suspects and prospects may be identified for TAMs by national promotional campaigns, by sales referral, or by customers calling direct. This information should be converted into the lists from which a TAM works.

Just as no perfect account manager

exists, no perfect salesperson exists. The skills required for a good salesperson are similar to those required for account management. Typically, new business salespeople, responsible for opening new accounts, need to be high on activity and time management skills. They need the activity rate of a new business salesperson combined with the skills of the account manager!

Channels of distribution and of communication

One symptom of increased customer orientation is the highlighting of how a company manages and communicates with its customers. One aspect of this is the channel through which it deals with those customers. This may be a direct sales force, a distributor, dealer or agent, a sales office, telemarketing unit, or a retail outlet.

Formally defined, a *channel of distribution* is the method a company uses to get its products and services to customers and to manage relationships with them before and after the sale.

Channels can be defined *physically*. This covers:

- the way a product is transported to a customer, perhaps via a third party
- how the product is stored while it is waiting to be bought
- how the customer comes in physical contact with the supplier

Channels can also be defined *commercially*. This relates more to the business process at work, and covers:

- how customers are identified or how they identify themselves
- how they come into commercial contact with the supplier

- how transactions take place
- how they are completed
- how customers are managed after the sale

Companies use different channels of distribution to manage different types of customers. We have already considered the use of key account salespeople to handle large customers and dealers to handle smaller customers. In some cases, it may be the type, rather than size, of customer that is important. For example, some companies use channels which are specialized in the needs of particular industry sectors. However, in all cases, the type of channel chosen should be closely supported by marketing communications policy.

A *channel of communication* is closely related to a channel of distribution, but not the same. It is the means you use to get information about your company and its products and services to your customers. It is also the means you use to receive information about what your customers' needs are, and how your customers would like to be dealt with. The main challenges in communication channel management are:

- what mix of communication media to use (e.g. TV, radio and press advertising, direct mail, business centres, exhibitions, seminars, etc.)
- who you should be communicating with
- what messages to send via these channels (e.g. should you be sending messages about individual products, or about ranges of products and services that meet identified needs)
- how often you should send these messages
- what information you should receive from customers via these channels
- how you ensure that the different messages you send do not clash, but are consistent with each other and properly sequenced

23

- how should you co-ordinate the different channels of communication so as to support distribution channels in their work – you may want to use several channels to influence a particular kind of customer, each channel playing a specific role at particular stages in your 'contact strategy'
- how to ensure that your company's overall brand is properly developed and supported, while promotions for products and services are as effective as possible
- how to do all this cost-effectively

TAMs have a key role to play in communicating with customers. Customers will see their communication with them as part of wider communication. This wider communication includes coupons they have filled in to respond to campaigns, visits to showrooms, or commercials they have seen on television or in the press. This means that you need to understand the objectives and rationale of your company's communication with customers.

You also need to convey, through your handling of customers, a style which is consistent with the other messages the customer is receiving. This means that you must be kept up to date with what messages the customer has received, and how they have been asked to respond to them. Ideally, all direct communication from your company to telemanaged customers should appear to come from TAMs. This provides strong endorsement of the communication and makes it much more effective. Hence the need for a high degree of co-ordination and investment in the right systems.

Ideally, your TAM operation should be established as a main (or the sole) sales channel for identified groups of customers. TAMs should have accountability for particular customers. They should be supported by highly relevant and

effective communications campaigns. If all this is achieved, then you should find that the information flows between the TAM operation and other parts of the marketing operation should be easy to create. For example, your advertising department should want to involve the TAM operation in its campaign planning, as well-informed TAMs will be able to make advertising expenditure effective. They do this by developing customers' interest which has been stimulated by the advertising.

When a TAM operation works mainly in a support role to other channels (e.g. key account management), however, it is more likely to be left out of the communications loop. You must therefore ensure that formal links are created between marketing and the TAM operation. These links must be well-managed, with a proper service agreement between the TAM operation and account management, specifying roles and responsibilities, briefing standards and communication requirements.

Database marketing

As we saw in Chapter 1, TAM depends for its success on the use of database and direct-marketing disciplines in communicating with customers – your company should be committed to database marketing principles. These imply the development of a high-quality customer database, carrying details of:

- your customers – who and where they are, what their characteristics are
- their needs
- their transactions with you (what they buy from you and what communication has passed between you)

Your company should also be committed to direct marketing principles. These

24

include the development of a structured and co-ordinated flow of communication between you and your customers, and should cover all advertising media, be properly targeted and timed, and promote the right offers which are expressed in language that customers understand, highlighting the benefits the offer will bring them. Each campaign should be based on thorough testing of each element of the campaign.

TAM therefore uses the database marketing approach – but what exactly does this involve? Database marketing is an interactive approach to marketing. It uses individually-addressable communications media (such as mail, telephone and the sales force) to:

- extend help to its target audience
- stimulate their demand
- stay close to them by recording and keeping an electronic database memory of customer, prospect and all communication and commercial contacts
- help improve all future contacts
- ensure realistic planning of all marketing

The central idea of database marketing is to ensure that you are driven by customers' needs. This is the very opposite of much selling, where customers are driven by your need to sell them products. However, to be driven by individual customer needs, you need to know who your customers are. You also need to establish direct communication with them. It is apparent why TAM is so closely connected to the database marketing approach.

The dialogue with customers

Database marketing improves the relationship with customers and prospects by:

- reaching them
- selling to them
- informing them
- listening to them
- conditioning them
- helping them communicate with us

A good marketing plan will normally contain a number of plans for communicating with customers, each constituting one or more campaigns (see below). A *campaign* consists of a period of structured communication. During a campaign, a customer receives one or more communications, and responds to them. The end result, usually a sale, is achieved. After a time, when all expected responses are in, the campaign is closed.

Your relationship with customers, however, should not just be a series of campaigns, unconnected with each other and interrupted by long periods of silence. You should not just talk to your customers only when you want to sell them something. This will reduce your chance of selling to them. It will also ensure that your customers are not very satisfied with you.

Your relationship with customers should be a true relationship. In this relationship, you should manage customers to achieve mutual benefit and satisfaction. The campaign is just a tool to focus your communications effort. This includes media advertising, direct marketing, public relations, exhibitions and sales force visits. Customers who are managed by TAMs should perceive that these interwoven threads of communication are simply an extension of their normal relationship with their TAM. The TAM, who is in charge of that relationship, should structure the dialogue with your customers based on knowledge of other communications and weave them into that dialogue. Otherwise, the relationship with the customer will become fragmented. Eventually, the data collected by TAMs will be the main basis for deciding which communication goes to which customers on what subjects.

From a database marketing perspective, the dialogue with customers must be seen as a continuous series of campaigns, of which one, the TAM overall sales campaign, is never-ending. Campaigns aimed at selling particular products and services start with identification or confirmation of customers needs. They end with a series of contacts which yield profit for your company and satisfaction for customers. Every distribution and communications channel – including TAM – plays a key role in this. Each channel used in a campaign should move customers closer to the purchasing decision. Each should also yield information to help you handle the customer better. This is also, in essence, how the TAM works.

What responses do you want from customers?

In database marketing, the response you seek from customers at each stage of your relationship varies. It may be a move to the next stage in the sales cycle. Responses we might be seeking at different stages include:

- placing an order
- information enabling you to qualify a respondent as a prospect
- commitment to an appointment with sales staff
- commitment to attendance at an exhibition, showroom or a sales seminar
- assurance that a prospect has received all relevant information about a product or service – this enables the salesperson to concentrate on selling
- indication of a favourable disposition to buy from your company

- acknowledgement of receipt and acceptance of messages which deliver branding information or support

Customers benefit from a well-planned sales dialogue with you because:
- they have the information they need to take decisions
- their problems may be solved before they occur
- they can make buying decisions with the confidence that they have obtained the right information and developed a good relationship with the supplier, which will ensure that the purchase goes smoothly

The two-way flow of information

Database marketing depends on the collection, maintenance and regular use of information about customers. A TAM operation can supply and check information about customers. However, if the information that the TAMs have to hand when making the call is not good quality, then the ability of TAM to achieve its information and cost-effectiveness objectives will be reduced. TAM works best with high-quality information. This applies particularly to information about customers and their needs. Since the TAM will normally have more frequent contact with his customers than anybody else in the company, the data gathered during his dialogue must be added to the database.

If the TAM concept is introduced in a company which already uses the database marketing approach, then at first the TAM will be very dependent on the quality of information on the company's database. This information may itself have been collated from other company databases – sales order entry, customer service, etc. Later on, much of the information about customers who are managed by TAMs will have been gathered

and/or checked by the TAMs themselves.

We cannot overemphasize the need for
a good customer database. It must
support tracking of contacts with customers and allow campaign modelling.
It should be the *sole* marketing database,
containing information (provided by *all*
marketing and sales groups) about
customers, the types of marketing action
you have taken with them and how they
have responded. This is critical in
managing your relationships with customers proactively.

A proper customer marketing database
also allows marketing staff to assess the
effectiveness of previous campaigns,
and to target future campaigns more
accurately. It is another virtuous circle.
The more the customer database is used,
with customer information and dialogue
information being keyed back into the
system, the more accurate the data
becomes. The more accurate the data,
the more able are the sales and
marketing teams to address relevant
sales and marketing activities to the
customers (right time, right offer, right
place). If this happens, the more the
system will be used . . . and so on. This
should result in better, more lasting
business between your customers and
your company.

In a multi-channel company, the marketing database may be fed by a variety of
operational systems used by different
channels to run their daily activities. But
the feed must be frequent (ideally on-
line or at least overnight processing). A
modular approach to operational systems ensures that operational integrity is
not compromised by marketing needs.

We use the idea of the *contact strategy* to
manage the customer relationship. A
contact strategy is a particular set of
steps used in handling a customer. It
starts with the initial contact and goes
through to the conclusion of the

particular phase in the dialogue, when
the customer has either agreed to meet
your objective (e.g. a purchase) or
decided not to. You will use different
contact strategies to manage your
customers through to the sale. For
example, you might decide that a
particular customer may need more
information, so you need a letter asking
them whether they are interested. If they
are, you send a brochure. You then make
a follow-up call and try to close. If the
service you are trying to sell is very
complex, you may ask the field salesperson to make a face-to-face call. You
will choose contact strategies according
to the type of customer, their response
to your call, and the type of product.
Note that your TAMs will also be one
element of the contact strategy for some
campaigns.

We formalize contact strategies, by
having well-prepared options to deal
with different turns which our dialogue
with customers might take, to produce:

- clearer options for customers, e.g.
  not 'Do you want more information?'
  but 'May I send you our brochure?'
  or 'Would you like our sales
  representative to call or to come to
  our next sales seminar on topic X?'
- economies of scale, e.g. standard
  brochure, sales seminar where a
  dialogue with several customers can
  be conducted at once
- control over fulfilment, e.g. if you
  have a standard brochure or regularly scheduled seminars, the process of informing the customer can
  be handled fairly automatically

In a TAM operation, all campaign-driven
activities should be integrated with TAM
activities. One of the prime functions of
the database marketing approach is to
co-ordinate the different sales and
marketing approaches to your customers. This ensures that there is a high
degree of uniformity in your approach.
It ensures that customers receive the

communication that suits them, for the offer that suits their needs, at the right time. In some campaigns, the TAM may feature as one of the contact routes, whether for the outbound first contact or the inbound response, depending on the customer's need.

The campaign process

Campaign design

TAMs can function as one part of a wider campaign, but they also lead their own campaigns – the 'everlasting' customer sales campaign designed to yield ever-increasing sales.

The design of the TAM campaign depends on:

- how long the TAM concept has been used in your company
- how your customers and staff have worked with it
- the kind of customers you have
- the products you sell

First, suppose you are using TAM to deal with customers who may have bought from you in the past, but with whom you have no regular contact, Here, in the early stages of TAM implementation, it may be best to keep campaigns simple. You should focus on a few basic products you are certain these customers need. This will help build confidence in staff (that they know how to do it) and customers (that you are making the right offer to them). Then, as the relationship develops, a wider range of products and services can be offered.

Another approach would be to produce a broad catalogue of items and let customers' needs drive the dialogue. However, if your products are techni-cally complex, this approach may require too much product training for TAMs before you go live. Therefore, you may decide to concentrate on a limited range. In this case, your initial contacts with customers will appear product campaign-oriented. After a number of contacts, and more TAM training, the customer will be fully in tune with the TAM process. It may well be necessary to continue the campaign approach into the future. But by this stage any approach to the customer base will be truly integrated with the TAM methodology.

Second, suppose you are implementing the TAM approach with a well-established customer base (e.g. if you are changing the channel from field sales to TAM). In this case, you may want to – and customers will probably expect you to – start with the full range of products. You may need to spend much time on earlier calls doing an in-depth diagnosis of customer needs. This will enable the TAM to gather all the information required to sell the full range. However, if your product range is very wide, you may start TAMs off with a limited product range, gradually increasing their product coverage with time, and using field sales staff less.

In working with the TAMs in these ways, you will need to draw upon some of the principles of database marketing campaign design. The elements of campaign design are usually summa-rized as follows:

- *Targeting* – Targeting relates to who we call. Even the best designed campaign will yield bad results if we aim it at the wrong customers.
- *Timing* – Timing relates to when we contact the customer. We can get this wrong if we ignore the customer's buying cycles (e.g. replacement demand, business expansion or moving, seasonality, or personal availability – i.e. freedom to take a call). Targeting and timing, taken

- together, are 'customer-side' variables. They relate to our ability to identify our market.
- *The offer* – The offer is what product or products we are promoting to the customer. It includes any packaging and incentives. These elements are combined, so as to meet customer needs. The offer is a critical factor in encouraging the customer to buy.
- *Creative* – The creative is the way in which we express the offer. In a telemarketing campaign, the creative is the 'script' or 'call guide'. The call guide is critically important in TAM. It ensures that we have made the right contact, at the right time, with the right product, that the data from the contact comes back to us, and that when TAMs make the call they feel professional about what they are doing. The offer and the creative, taken together, are 'supplier-side' variables. They relate to our ability to put together the right package for the market. The competitive advantage of TAM is that it leads to many more of the right customers being contacted personally at the right time, with the right offer expressed in the right way.

The TAMs should provide most of the information needed to ensure that the campaign is successful. During each sales cycle with an individual customer, the TAM should ask questions designed to find out when the next sales cycle should begin (timing) for that customer (targeting). The TAM should also ask which products the customer is likely to be interested in (the offer). The creative (the call guide) should be adapted by them to fit the needs of the relationship established with that customer.

respond to customer needs at the time they are expressed. In database marketing, we call this *enquiry management*. It applies whether you make the call to the customer, or vice versa. When customers enquire about a product, their interest in it is usually more than transitory. The interest will not disappear if you do not respond instantly. But the customer may be making similar enquiries of your competition. If you respond quickly and appropriately, you stand a better chance of making the sale. This is not just because you impress your customers with your professionalism. If you present your 'case' first, it will have greater impact. Also, if you train your TAMs well, so that they can identify all sales opportunities and exploit them there and then – however the conversation started – you will achieve higher levels of productivity.

When TAMs call customers, or vice versa, good enquiry management involves the following:

- Quickly extracting from the customer the information which enables the TAM to decide which products or services are of interest or are most suitable, now and in the future, and what the next step in managing the enquiry should be, taking into account the customer's expressed preferences concerning your response.
- Telling the customer what the next step will be.
- Implementing the next step quickly.
- Deciding the remaining steps in handling the enquiry.
- Setting in motion the mechanism which will deliver these steps, including prioritization of enquiries.

Enquiry management

A strength of TAM is the ability to

Fulfilment

The term *fulfilment refers to the process*

29

by which the enquiry is managed to the point where the customer is satisfied with the conclusion. Fulfilment may consist of a number of further steps. These include sales visits, telephone calls, invitations to a showroom, sales seminar or exhibition, or an order for the product. There are many different routes an enquiry can take. We may wish to deploy different types of response handling techniques, according to the type of customer and response. In some cases, the TAM will be part of the fulfilment mechanism for national campaigns. In other cases, they will be the dominant part of the fulfilment, e.g. if a customer calls the TAM to place an order.

Testing

To get the best response, we test different approaches. The key element to be tested in the TAM's work is the call-guide. This assists the TAM in conducting the conversation with the customer. The TAM may want to test such things as whether the presentation of the offer is right for the product and target market or whether the guide helps to identify needs properly. Without a call guide, it would be impossible to test the creative at all.

Targeting

Your ability to manage your dialogue with customers depends on two kinds of targeting:

- *market targeting* – identifying the kinds of needs which you can satisfy
- *individual targeting* – selecting individual customers who have these needs

Good targeting depends on the informa-

tion on the database being high quality and on using the right criteria for selecting customers for a campaign. When you use the database to select customers for a campaign, you need to define a *target customer profile*. This indicates the kind of customer you want to attract with the campaign. It gives you the criteria by which to select customers from the database. Selection is facilitated by your ability to control your target precisely. Controlling your selection criteria enables you to test the responses of different types of customer to different approaches. For example, you might discover by testing that for a particular product and target market, a visit to a showroom increased sales level more than enough to justify the cost of the visit. You would then build the visit invitation into the campaign in question.

Management disciplines

All database marketing activities require tightly controlled, systematic measurement and management. Database marketing is often justified by its accountability – it can genuinely claim to know when a campaign is cost-effective, because all inputs and outputs are measured. Both these points apply with equal force to TAM.

Branding

The term *branding* refers to how you want your customers to perceive your company and/or products and the images you would like them to associate with you. Branding is a vital component of marketing strategy. Wherever supporting your company's brand(s) demands a level of closeness to the customer, frequency of contact and consultative selling which cannot be achieved economically by a direct sales force, you should consider the TAM solution. To achieve this, however, the TAM must be trained to translate these values into values that are relevant for the different types of customer at the other end of the line. These may be a senior secretary, a purchasing manager, a marketing director or a managing director. Thus, if your company branding is to be a leader in your field, then you must provide your TAMs with up-to-date information on relevant developments of the kind that will interest all the customer staff your TAMs are likely to talk to.

Some companies are naturally concerned about exposing staff who may be quite junior and new to the company to a wide range of contacts in customer companies. They are not sure whether TAMs will be able to sustain the degree of professionalism which branding requires. However, one of the agreeable aspects about most customers is that they are inherently reasonable – provided they are treated well! They do not expect an instant answer to everything. A TAM should not therefore be expected to provide information on every product and service immediately. No reasonable customer will expect this. They will, however, expect the TAM to deal with their needs professionally, and come back to them with a reasoned recommendation, well thought through and presented over the phone. This is the true meaning of professionalism in a TAM. If you go into a shop to buy a new domestic appliance, such as a washing machine, how do you feel if the salesperson answers all your questions immediately, without referring to any promotional material and without stopping to think? Are you impressed by the salesperson's skill, or do you wonder if the answers are being made up on the spot?

There is of course no right or wrong approach. The key message is try to provide what customers need. If they need a quick response, you may want to give it to them, but agree that you will check it out in more detail.

Telemarketing

Telemarketing involves using the telephone as a properly managed part of the marketing, sales and service mix. It differs from telephone selling – teleselling – which is aimed at getting sales over the telephone. Teleselling is usually used as a stand-alone strategy rather than an integrated element of the marketing mix. In business-to-business marketing, telemarketing has been used for many years. In consumer marketing, teleselling is still very common, but telemarketing is beginning to be adopted.

Many businesses and consumers find teleselling a nuisance. Consumers have a ready set of excuses to deal with poorly targeted calls: 'I've got one already' or 'We had it done last year' must be the commonest. In business, such calls are often barred by secretaries, acting on their managers' instructions. TAM is right at the other extreme. TAM is telemanaging *your* customers. You already have a relationship with them, and they with you. You are unlikely to be barred!

- Telemarketing is a discipline in the fullest sense of the word. It involves the use of telecommunications equipment and networks by highly trained staff. Their aim is to achieve your company's marketing objectives by carrying out a controlled dialogue with customers who need the benefits provided by your company. In so doing, they are supported by systems which allow your company to manage the workflow, measure it and follow through the outcome of the dialogue.

- Telemarketing requires systematic management, measurement and control of every aspect of its operation. Without this, you would not know the relationship between the inputs of a telemarketing operation. This information is essential if you are to achieve effectiveness.
- Telemarketing is growing quickly. Costs of contacting and managing customers by other means (e.g. the field sales force) are rising. We are learning more about why and when customers are happy to do business over the telephone, and putting this knowledge to work. Customers find the telephone a cost-effective way of learning about and buying a company's products and services.

Customers find the telephone one of the best ways of conducting their relationships with their suppliers because:

- *The telephone saves their time.* They do not have to handle the formality of a sales visit, or travel to see the product.
- *The telephone allows them to feel they control the relationship.* They can tell you when it is convenient to call, and call you when convenient to them. They can terminate the call when they want.
- *The telephone gives them information when they need it.* They may find it frustrating to wait for information to come in the post or during a field sales visit. They can call you and you can respond immediately or quite soon after.
- *The telephone gives them a direct dialogue with you.* This gives them confidence in the relationship.

The telemarketer (and TAM is one) should remind customers of these advantages and reinforce them by ensuring that every call is a high-quality experience!

Key concepts in telemarketing

Telemarketing is best employed as an aspect of database marketing. A key principle of database marketing is that we need to be in constant dialogue with our customers. This ensures that their needs are being met and that the information on the database is kept fresh. In a dialogue, information flows both ways. Through TAM, you become committed to a dialogue with your customer. This dialogue lasts as long as you keep the customer. It will consist in a series of 'conversations', conducted over the telephone. Letters, brochures and other material confirm or add to what is said. A sales visit or visit to a showroom takes place where necessary.

We distinguish two types of call – *inbound* (calls customers make to us) and *outbound* (calls we make to customers). In Table 3.1, we identify which marketing and sales tasks we believe are best carried out by each mode.

The objective of the TAM is to achieve a managed dialogue, consisting of a progressive series of conversations focused on customer needs. The dialogue is being managed in a certain way at particular times. Each conversation is targeted to achieve specific sales cycle objectives – gathering information or presenting options.

Conversations tend to have specific objectives in terms of conveying information and/or moving the customer forward one or more stages in the buying cycle. The vast majority of TAM calls should be outbound, reflecting the proactive management of the dialogue. To maintain the cost-effectiveness of the approach, these calls are not made at the convenience of the TAM. They are either scheduled at a time the customer has said is convenient, or they may be

Table 3.1 TAM activities

Activity	Outbound	Inbound	TAM suitability*
Call reception		×	3
Enquiry handling		×	2
Enquiry qualification	×	×	1
Customer (market) research	×		2
Product research	×		3
List cleaning/enhancement	×		2
Complaint handling		×	3
Information dissemination	×		2
Order taking	×	×	1
Cross/up selling	×	×	1
Lead generation	×		2
Servicing marginal accounts	×	×	1
Progress chasing	×		2
Account management/development	×	×	1
After-sales customer care	×		1

Task suitability.
1 = TAM is particulary suited, 2 = TAM might be required to do occasionally, 3 = TAM should do rarely.

programmed by TAM support staff under management supervision, to maximize the effectiveness of the day's workflow.

Telemarketing in context

Telemarketing, and in particular TAM, helps us achieve many objectives. They may be fundamental, 'coal-face' objectives, i.e. what particular 'customer-facing' staff should do with individual customers. Or they may be higher-level, more strategic objectives. Here are some examples:

'Coal-face' objectives

1 Progressing the relationship with the customer

- *Call handling* – answering customer calls on any matter, whether enquiries about products, requests for service, handling complaints or problems.
- *Moving toward a sale* – lead generation, appointment creation, order-taking, seeking or closing, selling up or cross-selling, converting non-sales-related inbound or outbound calls into sales opportunities.
- *Cold calling* – normally as part of a campaign.
- *Building loyalty* – by meeting needs and by just listening and remaining in contact.

2 Obtaining or providing information

- *Enquiry screening* – obtaining information to confirm whether a customer is a prospect for a product, or how serious a particular problem is.
- *Customer and market research* – gathering information to use in making business decisions; this includes screening of lists of customers or

33

prospects to be used in particular marketing campaigns.

- *Delivering customized advice.*

Strategic objectives

- *Account management* – improving the quality of account management, so certain groups of customers benefit from a better relationship with the organization, e.g. finding new purchasers within existing accounts, preventing competitive inroads into customers, and reactivating lapsed customers.
- *New business* – identifying and developing new customers and new markets, extending coverage of existing markets, or launching a new product or service.
- *Quality* – improving the effectiveness, professionalism and economics of the sales force and other channels.
- *Customer care* – improving customer service and satisfaction.

Summary

In summary then, where does TAM management fit?

- *Customer-oriented marketing* – TAM is the key to providing high levels of customer service to certain customers.

- *Account management* – Telephone account management is the most cost-effective way to handle certain customers.

- *Channels of distribution and communication* – All commercial relationships with certain customers can be handled by TAMs, as can person-to-person communication.

- *Selling* – TAMs are first and foremost sales staff. They use account management disciplines over the telephone to achieve sales. Achievement of improved customer satisfaction is one of the main routes to more sales, but the account manager must make the sale.

- *Database marketing* – TAM must work to database marketing disciplines.

- *Campaigns* – Whatever marketing communication campaigns you run, your TAM operation must be closely integrated with them.

- *Branding* – TAM can provide excellent support for your company's branding, or destroy it!

- *Telemarketing* – Provides the fundamental technical and sales disciplines within which TAM works.

4

The TAM operation

The workings of the TAM operation will now be described in broad terms. The details of the operation and the daily processes will be described fully in following chapters. The TAM operation can be discussed in terms of the following:

- the TAM process
- target markets and products
- integration within the marketing organization
- lists
- call strategy
- call guides
- targets and budgets
- management

The TAM process

Before any customer can be called, you must set up your TAM operation so that the TAMs can start their daily routine. Setting up the operation is described fully in Chapter 5. However, setting up is just the first step in running the operation. Here is an overview of all the steps involved.

Set up

The TAM process is set up. Systems are

installed. The database is set up. Staff are recruited and trained. These include support staff, who do the administrative work, and allow the TAMs to concentrate on selling. Product and relationship campaigns are decided upon. Call guides are provided, tailored to the customers and products which are the subject of the campaign.

List extraction

A customer list is generated from your company's customer database. Lists are selected using criteria provided by TAM management, probably in consultation with other people in your marketing department. For example, if you are using TAMs to deal only with companies of a certain size, and are allocating customers by area, then the selection criteria will be company size and area. The customer database should provide the information in the form of a contact record for each customer. These are headed by a selection of the information that the database holds about that customer. The rest is a form which is filled in by the TAM (on screen or on paper) while making the call. The fact that each name has been provided should be recorded on the customer database, as this information will be used in campaign planning. It also

35

allows statistics to be generated about customers who are being managed by TAMs.

Calling starts

Individually, TAMs begin to progress their relationship with their customers in a step-wise manner. The mix of activities during the working day will differ, but each activity is part of a well thought-out and highly controlled process for managing the relationship with the customer. Here is a step-by-step description of the process:

(i) Each day, each TAM receives a day file from the supervisor or from the computer which runs the TAM operation, depending on the degree of automation. This file may be provided on paper or on screen. Information on customers who are already TAM-managed is provided together with past contact records. Initial contact records are provided on new TAM customers.

(ii) TAMs make calls to their customer from their day file (see above).

(iii) The first call would be part of the campaign to introduce the customer to the TAM concept. Later calls are fixed by agreement with the customer and according to whether the customer is targeted for another campaign.

(iv) Leads are passed to the TAM as a result of inbound enquiries that have come in through other routes.

(v) Account-managed customer calls (inbound) are handled by the support staff, who pass the information to the TAM. If necessary, the TAM then makes an outbound customer call. If no support staff are provided, these calls are handled by the TAM, but this may weaken the TAM's sales efforts.

(vi) If the call is an outbound call, and there is no answer or the number is engaged, another call is scheduled by the TAM for the same day. If there is still no answer, checks are made to establish whether there is a list error if the number has been provided from the customer database. If the number is still engaged, the call is rescheduled and handled as above.

(vii) If a contact is made, but not with a decision-maker, the TAM asks to be referred to the decision-maker. If this request is refused, then the call is terminated and rescheduled to a later date. If the decision-maker is found not to be available, the TAM establishes when it would be convenient to call, and the call is rescheduled. If the decision-maker is outside the TAM's area of responsibility (e.g. different geographical area or another company), the call is terminated and the information passed on to the appropriate sales group. If the decision-maker is available, then the call may be transferred or the TAM may call the decision-maker direct.

(viii) Results of calls are coded on a form (in the paper-based approach) or picked up by the computer. Calls where the decison-maker has not been contacted may be concluded in a variety of ways. It may be that there is no contact with the target decision-maker or gatekeeper (someone who handles access to the decision-maker). The line may have been engaged. The call may be reprogrammed for later. A gatekeeper may have been contacted, and a recall arranged for the decision-maker. The TAM may conclude that there has been a list error, perhaps because the target number is uncontactable. The decision-maker may be on another site, or may not be located in the right area (e.g. if TAM territories are split on geographical lines). Finally, there may have been a simple misdial.

(ix) If the decision-maker is contacted, the TAM asks a series of questions relating to their needs, following the relevant call guide. The information resulting from answers to these questions is recorded for use in future calls and for handling subsequent actions in relation to the current call. Without this information being recorded, it would be impossible to schedule follow-up outbound calls properly. This would drastically reduce the cost-effectiveness of TAM.

(x) If a paper-based system is being used, most of this information should be entered on forms, which are processed by support staff. If the process has been automated, most information will be entered directly by the TAM onto the system.

(xi) If the decision-maker has been contacted then a number of outcomes are possible: (a) The customer may have decided to buy the product(s), so a contract or confirmation will need to be sent to the customer; (b) the customer may want to be account-managed, but does not want to buy now; (c) the customer may never want to be contacted by you; (d) the customer may have non-sales needs (e.g. service); (e) the customer may require more information; (f) a quotation may be requested; (g) the decision-maker may not have been ready to decide yet, and a call back may have been scheduled; (h) a lead may have been generated for a salesperson to call on the customer; (i) the customer may want a demonstration of a product or service.

(xii) If the customer requires further standard information, and if your company uses a fulfilment house to send out literature, the customer database is used to ensure that the fulfilment house is informed. The customer is then contacted later to progress the sale. A follow-up call is scheduled later for this reason. The fulfilment house which handles all the literature sent out in this way is notified through the customer database. The fulfilment house will already have taken a sample signature of the TAM, which will automatically be added to the customized version of the standard letter accompanying the literature.

(xiii) If a standard letter cannot be sent, the TAM may ask the support team to send literature directly. Typically, this will happen for a multiple product request, or requests specific to that customer, e.g. quotations or contracts. Typically, fulfilment houses can only handle straightforward standard responses and should be used wherever possible in this way.

(xiv) If the customer wishes to discuss more complex product and services, face-to-face contact may be organized. This might be a visit to a showroom or a visit by field sales staff. The contact record is coded accordingly.

(xv) The results of this stage of the relationship are notified to the database. Possible results include a sale of the target product, sale of another product, or no sale but call back after a certain period.

(xvi) The TAM (or the computer) updates the dialling record for every dial made, entering the campaign code and the outcome of the dial.

(xvii) The next call is scheduled.

(xviii) The support team collects all the contact records that have been processed by the team and files them, together with those that have had contracts raised. Some files are date and TAM sequenced, to allow follow-up by a particular TAM on a particular day. Others are archived in customer name order. The support team cross-checks dialling records and contact records, to ensure that dialling record figures are correct. If your system is computerized, all this will be done automatically.

These steps are obviously a simplified version of the process, but it covers nearly every eventuality. The aim should be to automate as much of this process as possible, allowing TAMs to focus all their energy and time on talking to customers in a relevant and disciplined way.

To maintain cost-effectiveness, as many sales steps as possible should be carried out within one call. Hence, the importance of proper targeting and timing. The customer should be ready to buy when the TAM calls. You will only know when this is if you ensure that, as part of each call, you find out when the customer will next be ready to buy!

Target markets and products

As discussed earlier, your marketing strategy will determine which of your products and services TAMs will be selling into which markets, and should be part of the business plan which you put forward to justify the investment in TAM. The returns you make to your TAM investment will depend upon the following:

- *Products* – This refers to the breadth of the product range sold by TAMs and the amount of profit margin available on products. The broader the product range, the greater the initial training and scripting investment, but the earlier and greater the returns from cross-selling.
- *Target market* – This refers to the size of the target market addressed. The greater the target market, the higher the potential sales volume, but the more varied the type of customer you will be addressing. This may mean greater investment in list cleaning and TAM training.
- *Competition* – If competitive pressures are intense, then deploying TAMs should prevent losses in revenue and profit.

Given the learning curve that TAMs and their management must go through, it makes sense to focus first on products and markets which are of high priority, and then broaden out the approach later on. However, this is subject to a major qualification. Beware of starting with markets that need the full range of skills and product and service knowledge. It is better to start with a small range of products and with accounts that have relatively simple needs. When your TAMs have been through their learning curve with these customers, they should be ready to embark on the more difficult learning involved in selling complex products to complex customers!

Integration within the marketing organization

For an established business, introducing TAM may have significant implications for staff previously involved in handling customers now to be handled by TAMs. Ideally, the TAM approach will fit in neatly, like a piece in a jigsaw, with the other distribution and communication approaches your company uses. The effective use of the TAM approach depends strongly on co-operative working with these other areas of marketing and sales. TAMs will be the initiators of customer contacts in a situation where initiation was rare. The TAM team and its management will be working closely with them to ensure the delivery of a better service to customers. The introduction of this new element must be handled sensitively but confidently. The roles of existing channels may need to be modified to enable the jigsaw to fit properly. Also, this change may need to be phased in slowly.

Particularly in the early stages of TAM implementation, there is a great need to understand the plans of other marketing groups. Your TAM team must work with them and not against them. TAMs must be told of marketing initiatives before their customers are. The TAM operation should let others in sales and marketing know what the TAMs are doing, and how TAM actions can help others achieve their objectives. This internal PR and communications role is critical for the smooth introduction of the TAM concept.

In most companies, the units likely to be affected most by the introduction of TAM are the field sales force and sales offices which specialize in inbound call handling. The latter handle enquiries by customers, perhaps making the occasional outbound call to solicit orders or to make appointments for field sales staff. Retail or dealer/distributor operations may also be affected.

The sales office

In many businesses, a sales office fulfils various functions – customer management, sales force support, telemarketing and order-taking. Many sales office staff carry out one or two basic sales tasks.

These include:

- dealing with inbound sales enquiries
- fulfilment, to ensure that the customer gets what he wants (e.g. a product brochure, confirmation of order entry, delivery or installation)
- customer service enquiries

Normally, the field service and maintenance function will be handled separately. Many sales office staff feel their work is cut out just dealing with the existing volume of enquiries coming in.

The creation of TAM implies change. Those customers managed by TAMs will be taken away from sales offices. This transfer of responsibility means that staff working in sales offices will be able to streamline their activities considerably. They will be able to focus on the requirements of customers deemed not suitable for TAM. However, you may plan to phase out the sales office function entirely, retraining the staff to fulfil TAM roles. If so, you must be careful not to compromise on the recruitment requirements. Reactive sales office work is not an ideal qualification for the highly proactive life of a TAM!

If the sales office function is retained, the introduction of TAM may create a feeling of 'losing the plum job and the plum customers'. This must be handled diplomatically. TAMs require the full co-operation of sales offices in the hand-over period. They will need co-operation later, as customers may move across the boundaries of the two operations. For example, if TAMs are focused on larger customers, then sales offices may be handling smaller customers. As customers grow, they will move across the boundaries. Remember, customers are human beings. We may talk about them becoming a different category of customer, but all the customer wants is to continue to be handled professionally as they grow. Any change in the way they are handled must be explained carefully to them, in terms of the benefits to them.

The role of the TAM should always be primarily to sell, and not deal with customer service. If your products, services and customers are such as to generate a high volume of calls which are non-sales related queries and customer service calls, we advise that a specific resource be dedicated to handling these calls. If customers cannot easily differentiate these calls from sales-related calls, then the staff handling them should be located within the TAM operation or be provided with telecommunications systems which ensure very easy communication with it. They should in any case be provided with dedicated inbound-only telephone lines. If customers can easily differentiate these calls from sales-related calls, and the customer understands why a different unit should be called, then a separate unit can be set up to handle them. The inbound unit should be trained to diagnose when a TAM follow-up call is needed, and be able to schedule it with the customer ('My colleague [preferably named] will be calling you').

The field sales force

The effect of the introduction of TAM on your field sales force will also be significant. Some of the field sales force will no longer be directly accountable for customers handled by TAMs. Instead, they will be guided by your TAM operation. They may even be incorporated in it. However, the TAM operation must be allowed time to accustomize itself. The quality of the information on the customer database will need to be checked, and may involve anywhere from a couple of weeks to several months, depending on the quality of your database. You may decide to start

the TAM team off by allowing them to sell only those products which were neglected by the field sales force.

Therefore, for various reasons, it may not be right to make a drastic change, by complete withdrawal of some of the field sales force. In the early period of a TAM operation, drastic change should be avoided. A staged withdrawal may be better. This decision depends on whether you are actually reducing the number of field sales staff. If your TAM customers were badly neglected by field sales staff (too infrequent calling, perhaps due to lack of resource), then it will be easy to make the change without alienating customers. They will appreciate the difference. But if your sales force were calling too often (e.g. too small an average order size to justify the field calls), the change must be explained to customers.

The field sales staff concerned will be split into two groups. The first group will consist of those you are retraining to work as TAM field sales support. Their calling will be co-ordinated by TAMs. The second group will be transferred to other areas of responsibility (e.g. non-TAM customers). Those being retrained to work with TAMs must be evaluated-for their attitude to the change. Losing their much-prized independence can be resented. However, sales people who were frustrated by the quality of leads coming from existing marketing approaches may be excellent candidates for this new role.

TAM field sales staff work best with TAMs when they see the demonstrated benefit – to them – of so doing. This means better prospects and more sales. There is thus a high premium on ensuring that the field sales people become an integral part of the TAM team – though they may be focused on particular groups of customers. Their contribution will become more focused on those parts of the sales cycle which demand a face-to-face presence. These include:

- demonstrating a product
- gathering information which is difficult to gather over the telephone
- deepening contact with senior decision makers
- closing a difficult sale
- solving difficult product application problems

Note that a period with a TAM operation may be a useful prelude to a sales job with a full field sales force. The disciplined approach that will be learnt should be invaluable.

The TAM field sales people must be as disciplined in their calling as the TAMs are in theirs. They must follow the work plan given to them as the TAMs follow the call schedules given to them. Both types of staff have to work to the same disciplines. All this requires human beings to change what may be habits of a lifetime. Good management and training will be needed, but still there will be problems – so do expect them and legislate for them.

The high degree of automation involved in a TAM operation does not reduce the need for intelligent planning of sales calls. This is an area where TAM and field sales should work closely together. Doing so gives both the opportunity to use a wider range of skills.

Lists

For TAM to work effectively, outbound telephone calls must be co-ordinated with other sales activities. Your company's database marketing system should be its best source of marketing information. To generate lists from this system for use by your TAMs requires

that you first identify the customer characteristics by which you are going to be selecting customers for allocation to TAMs. Many selection criteria can be used to generate lists – location, products purchased, whether customers have responded to previous campaigns, etc. Later, when the TAM operation is fully set up, you will return to the marketing database for lists of customers. For example, you may want a list of all TAM customers who are likely to be prospects for a new product, based upon a national needs questionnaire which was entered onto the database. Figure 4.1 shows how this process works.

Call strategy

The call strategy applied in the TAM process must relate to the main tasks of the TAM. These are normally to cover the customer base proactively and to increase the revenue by selling needed products and services to the customer. TAM calls are of several kinds. They include:

- outbound from lists produced by a database marketing system
- outbound as a result of leads passed to the TAM from inbound enquiries from various sources
- outbound calls diarized as part of the account-management relationship
- inbound calls from telemanaged customers

The results of all calls must be accurately recorded for the process to work. At each stage the next activity, often dependent on the outcome of the current activity, should be determined in advance. This process is taken to its most detailed level in the generation of *call guides*. Through call guides, we make calling strategy work. Without the detail of the call guide, you cannot be sure that your

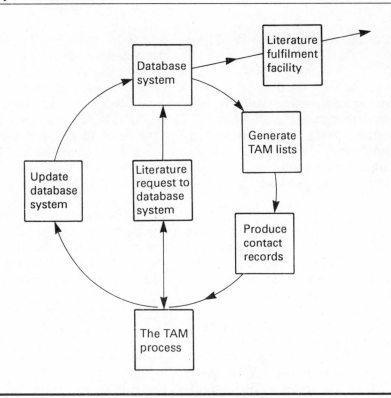

Figure 4.1 The database loops

strategy is being followed. The call strategy itself is determined by longer term objectives in managing the customer base. These usually relate to the kind of relationship you are trying to establish with your telemanaged customers. Though many call guides will relate to the sale of particular products and services, to be effective each must be compatible with the overall call strategy.

By having a series of related steps that conform to an overall strategy, the TAM builds up an active (and predetermined) business relationship with the customer. This relationship exists for the satisfaction (better, more focused support, service and solutions) of the customer. It also exists for the profit (more products/services sold to happier customers) of your company.

What makes the TAM process different from many other telemarketing functions is that the TAMs themselves are responsible for the complete process, up to and including closing the sale. The call strategy may well result in a sale (the most obvious conclusion), but must take into account the fact that the customer may not want to purchase immediately. Because the TAM approach gives such improved customer coverage, the call strategy must include a call-back option to keep the dialogue going. This continuous calling of customers, in a controlled way, is the essence of TAM.

Call guides

Call guides are a set of structured steps used to guide the telemanaged customer to a pre-determined conclusion. Call guides are used for a number of reasons, as follows:

- to promote the TAM service

- to gather information
- to probe customer needs for target/other products or services
- to make specific and relevant offers to answer needs
- to answer questions
- to tackle objections
- to close sales or take orders
- to probe for further potential

A call guide can be as simple as a logic diagram or as complete as a fully worded script. The idea of using call guides has been developed over many years. We recommend it for several reasons, outlined below.

- *Management input* – The experience, expertise and objective approach of management can be transmitted to the TAM by using these carefully thought-out guides. In this way, TAMs benefit from the experience of others. They will also have their actions (telephoning) directed towards a predetermined objective.
- *Ease of training* – Using structured guides, it is much easier to train TAMs. On-the-job coaching is also easier.
- *TAM confidence and professionalism–* Customers expect a calm, confident and professional approach from your company. The call guide can be used to overcome uncertainties when dealing with a new or different subject. It acts as a safety net when dealing with matters that seem – on the surface – to be well known. In either event, being prepared, and knowing what to say in any circumstances, invariably results in the caller sounding confident and relaxed.
- *Standardization without loss of techniques and skills* – By using a standard approach, all TAMs take the same line with customers. The line taken is consistent between calls to the same customer. A standard approach is reassuring to the customer. It also helps increase the level

of expertise and technique exercised by the TAM, through the extra confidence that it brings as well as the ease of training mentioned above.

- *Measurability* – In such a structured marketing operation, you must be able to accurately measure the results of any action taken. With a standard, scripted approach to telephone calling, you can measure the effects of each approach, as well as the effects of any changes in approach.
- *Customer relations* – The effect of this approach on customer relations is very positive. Increased professionalism and better techniques and skills result in a better dialogue with the customer. This leads to a long-term improvement in the relationship that you and your team have with the customer. This factor, coupled with the advantages of having a structured and predetermined call strategy, will be at the heart of your building a strong foundation from which to satisfy customer needs and enhance the revenue and profits of your company.

Targets and budgets

The TAM concept will deliver results only if certain productivity standards are met. By adhering rigidly to the structured approach to TAM, these standards should be attainable. The main TAM productivity standards, together with the numbers we believe to be feasible for dealing with all but the largest businesses are given below. For your particular business, of course, these numbers may be different.
- *Dials* – These are attempts to contact customers by placing a call. A target of 75–90 per day is reasonable.
- *Decision-maker contacts (DMCs)* – A

fully operational TAM should achieve 4,500 decision-maker contacts (DMCs) per year. This assumes that each TAM is fully operational for 36 weeks of the year (excluding training, leave and sickness), and at the telephone for 5 hours per day (i.e. 5 TAM telephone-hours per day). If they make 75–90 dials per day, and achieve a 'DMC: dials' ratio of 1:2.5 or 1:3, they should achieve approximately 25 DMCs per day, making 4500 per year.

- *Customers per TAM* – On average, a TAM can be effectively responsible for up to about 1100 customers, but this depends on how often you need to talk to customers.
- *Customer contacts* – This depends on the nature of your customers, products and services. It usually makes sense to arrange calls in call cycles, each composed of a series of calls. A call cycle is completed, or closed, when customers conclude that they will either buy or not buy from you. For example, 4500 DMCs per year with 1100 customers might be used to deliver an average of two cycles per customer of two calls each (four calls in all).
- *TAM costs* – In 1990, the average fully-loaded cost per TAM in the UK would be about £50 per TAM-hour. The equivalent figure in the USA would be about $140.
- *Revenues* – Revenues from TAM build up gradually as TAMs are trained to cover a broader range of products and services. Initially, TAMs need to spend a fair amount of their time building additional data about customers whose names have been provided by your database marketing system, and cleaning existing data. Their productivity may be quite low, and the operation may not be breaking even. Your TAMs will be learning, and their product range may be narrow. You should maintain your focus on call productivity and quality in the early

days – revenue and profit will follow.

Below are some examples of reasonable achievement figures in 1990, for the USA and the UK. Note that the implicit conversion ratios between the two countries differs. This is because US customers are more attuned to buying over the telephone. We hope UK figures will reach the same levels in a few years time.

At maturity, the revenue for campaign-driven inbound calls, plus cold calling outbound, might be £120 per TAM telephone-hour, or $360. This increases to around £600 ($1800) per TAM telephone-hour when lead conversion and inbound, fully account-managed calls are added. This increase will only be realized once the TAM unit is fully operational, probably after 18 months or more.

A few months after starting up, depending on your product, your TAMs may be generating around £100 per telephone-hour, or $300. In an industrial market, with small to medium customers (turnover of up to £30 million a year, or $50 million in the USA, this would be generated by about 100–125 decision-maker contacts (DMCs) per TAM per week. A TAM could be managing 1000 or so customers. For larger customers, revenue per telephone-hour might be greater. However, it may be generated by fewer DMCs (say 30–40 per week). Each TAM would handle fewer customers (say 100–200, and in some cases – for very large customers, i.e. over £500 million turnover, or $800 million in the USA – even fewer). Of course, if your relationship with customers is very close, or if your products are high revenue products, or bought intensely by your customers, you may achieve much higher figures.

Sales targets should be based on sales levels achieved from currently well-managed customers. These should be scaled up or down for the

- type of customer managed by the TAM
- the stage of the relationship
- the expertise of the TAM

Initial figures should have been worked out when the business justification for TAM was being put together, but targets must reflect the relatively slow take-off mentioned above. You should also frequently check the performance of your TAMs to assess the validity of such targets. The reporting systems required to log this information and analyse it are described in Chapter 8.

Management

Managing performance

We know that the TAM operation has to achieve a high level of motivation within a structured, controlled environment, so the skills needed to manage the group are very important. So too is the need to understand the key performance measurements required. The management skills in this environment (required specifically by the TAM's line manager) fall into three main areas:

- *Managing the TAM process* – This must be done from start to finish. It requires a full understanding of the process itself, and of the various marketing and management initiatives which are current within your company.

- *Managing and motivating people* – This element is critical. TAMs require significant attention in the early stages, to ensure that they are on the right track and that their motivation is kept at a high level. Involving the TAMs in management's measurement and control methods, and keeping them informed as to what outside initiatives are taking place – and how they are affected by these initiatives – help to maximize this motivation and to ensure an effective performance.

- *Coaching* – Coaching has two benefits for the team. First, on-the-job coaching improves technique and therefore performance. Second, coaching is a communications process. TAMs will feel much more involved (and therefore motivated) if their line manager spends time communicating with them.

Now that we have identified the main processes at work in a TAM operation, we need to show how a TAM operation should be set up.

5

Getting started

This discussion on how to set up a TAM operation is based on our experience and on a general model of life in a TAM environment. You will need to tailor it to your own requirements. How you do this depends upon:

- what facilities you have already – rooms, systems etc.
- your company's approach to installing new facilities and systems
- who is responsible for managing changes to facilities and systems
- the size of your proposed TAM operation.
- how quickly you need to implement it
- staffing constraints (numbers, grades, unions)
- employment standards
- your location

Accommodation

Starting with accommodation may seem prosaic, after the excitement of the previous chapters. But you *must* create the right environment for telemanaging. It is no use getting all the theory and systems right if your TAMs dislike their working environment. Skilled individuals who are highly trained in

marketing by telephone are very marketable themselves!

First, a comprehensive specification, covering all aspects of accommodation, facilities and furnishings, must be drawn up. This specification should be based on existing facilities where possible. A TAM operation should be established with the minimum of upheaval and expense. If you have some facilities already, try to adapt them, but do not compromise on the principles outlined below.

If you have one, consult with your estates or building services function. Together with them, develop the specification for your TAM operation, and begin to implement the plan.

Space requirements and overall design

A TAM operation needs the space in which to create a working environment incorporating a number of fixed features, but also designed to be flexible and free from distractions. All this often has to be done in a limited space. The TAM area must be self-contained, and must be isolated from through traffic or neighbouring departments. All dedicated

47

TAM staff should be accommodated in this area. The first line of the TAM operation (the 'Operations Manager' or TOM), the TAMs and their support staff must not be separated from each other. This would be highly inefficient and reduce the effectiveness of communication.

The TAM area and its furnishings and fittings must sustain motivation. The minimum area required for up to 12 staff (one manager, eight telephone account managers and three support staff) is approximately 140 square metres, with surrounding walls to physically isolate the group. TAMs must feel proud and happy to be in their environment. It should help them identify strongly with the company they represent. Furniture should *look* as if it represents a significant investment. It must appear almost tailor-made, rather than hurriedly put together. You must not create the impression that the TAM operation is cheap or second-rate. The impression created must sustain the status of the TAM operation in the eyes of senior management and the TAMs' colleagues – especially the field sales force.

It goes without saying that your company's standards for employee welfare – first aid, lavatories etc. – should be closely adhered to.

You must design a recreation area into the TAM operation's working space, which can be shared with associated groups such as field sales or sales office staff. Sharing with other groups working in closely related sales disciplines may prevent feelings of near-claustrophobia. Discussing different problems in relation to the same type of customers also provides insights. Recreation requires extra space on top of the 140 square metres mentioned above.

Job stress can be high in a TAM operation. Soft lighting will help reduce it. A 'clean' air-conditioning system will help reduce the spread of winter epidemics – a significant hazard in a full-time, desk-bound, enclosed job. If you can ensure a good supply of fresh air, even better, but this depends on location away from a noisy environment (main streets, flight paths, building sites).

Area and workstation design

A relatively noise-free environment should be achieved by using soft internal finishes such as carpets, window blinds, suspended ceilings and material-covered plasterboard partitions and walls (e.g. hessian or vinyl wall paper). They must be high quality, to support the TAMs' motivation. By using these materials, you ensure that noise is absorbed and that an atmosphere of calm is created, supporting the consultative selling approach that is so central to the telemanagement concept.

Within the TAM area, the TAM operations Manager needs a separate 'goldfish bowl' office. This must be sound-isolated from the rest of the operation, as this is where the TAM manager will coach TAMs individually. But it must also allow visual contact with the TAMs and other operational staff.

TAMs should each have their own workstation, which should be semi-isolated, with chest-high partitions. They should have adjustable work heights, to accommodate both sitting and standing while on the telephone.

Support staff also need workspace within the TAM area, sufficient for filing and sorting space for customer papers, as well as space for terminals, PCs and printers for the computer-based systems. Printers should be sited away from the TAMs if possible, to ensure that their noise will not interfere with conversations with customers. However, the ideal solution is to use laser printers.

Heating, ventilation and lighting must meet the highest standards. Your Office Services Manager or similar may help you here. If you do not have such a manager, consultants should be used to determine requirements. These will depend on factors such as the:

- location of the area you are using
- position of any windows
- number of people in the operation
- heat output of computer equipment
- positioning of workstations and computer terminals
- extent of existing services for heating, ventilation and lighting

Other furniture requirements

As well as the workstations needed for the TAMs, your support staff will need a desk each. Customer files should be kept in traditional hanging files. Space should be provided for items such as reports, brochures and stationery, and for storage and scheduling of contact records if your operation is paper-based. The TAM team will also need various chairs, desks and printer/VDU tables, as well as window blinds, whiteboards, flipchart easel, trays, sorters, waste bins and a wall-mounted planner. This is because many planning and training sessions will be held in the TAM area. The operation must also have easy access to a fast, high-volume, high-quality photocopier.

Systems

The electronic systems and equipment used in a TAM operation are of two main kinds – telecommunications-based and computer-based. The exact computer and telecommunication requirements will depend on the type of business you are in and the nature of those of your existing systems that need to be linked to the TAM operation.

If you can, pilot your TAM operation using a paper-based approach. Though this may be rather tortuous, and will never yield the productivity you will reach when fully automated, you will be much more likely to get things right in the end if you pilot the approach. You may opt for an interim approach, automating as much as possible with existing telecommunication and computing arrangements.

However you pilot, the customer must not see that it is a pilot. A well-prepared call, with all the information about the customer to hand, can be achieved with a paper-based system, or a computer-based system. In the former case, the details are spread on the desk in front of the TAM. In the latter case, they are on the screen. Although using a paper-based system, it will take the TAM longer to move between calls, this should not matter. The aim of a paper-based pilot should not be to establish the productivity levels that can be achieved with an automated approach! It is to establish such things as working practices and information requirements, and is also a good way to ensure that the automated system you specify really does meet the operation's needs.

All the TAMs and the various support and managerial staff will need telephones and a variety of support systems. Where possible, involve your in-house telecommunications and computer specialists in this project. They can advise on design and ordering of the systems and help with implementation and testing. Figures 5.1 and 5.2 show the telecommunications and computer systems of a typical TAM operation, and reference to them, in conjunction with the following, will provide further explanation.

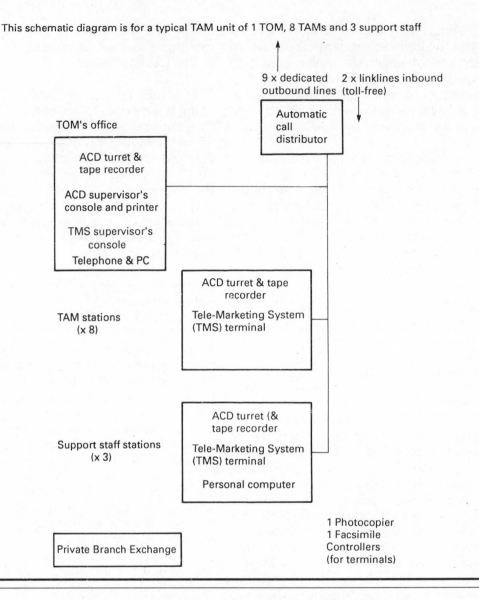

This schematic diagram is for a typical TAM unit of 1 TOM, 8 TAMs and 3 support staff

9 x dedicated   2 x linklines inbound
outbound lines (toll-free)

Automatic
call
distributor

TOM's office

ACD turret &
tape recorder

ACD supervisor's
console and printer

TMS supervisor's
console

Telephone & PC

ACD turret & tape
recorder

Tele-Marketing System
(TMS) terminal

TAM stations
(x 8)

ACD turret (&
tape recorder

Tele-Marketing System
(TMS) terminal

Personal computer

Support staff stations
(x 3)

1 Photocopier
1 Facsimile
Controllers
(for terminals)

Private Branch Exchange

Figure 5.1 Diagram of TAM installation

Telephony

The telephony requirements of TAMs are usually provided via an Automatic Call Distributor (ACD) or through Computer Integrated Telephony which can fully emulate all the features of ACD. There are devices now on the market which can be plugged straight into a standard private branch exchange to achieve this integration. An ACD is an independent unit which allows calls to be distributed between call receivers on a variety of programmed bases. It also enables the TAM Operations Manager to monitor each TAM's inbound and outbound telephone usage (since it provides printed statistics). This helps in monitoring TAMs against their targets for dials, decision-maker contacts, etc. It also enables the manager to listen in on – and record – any TAM conversation at

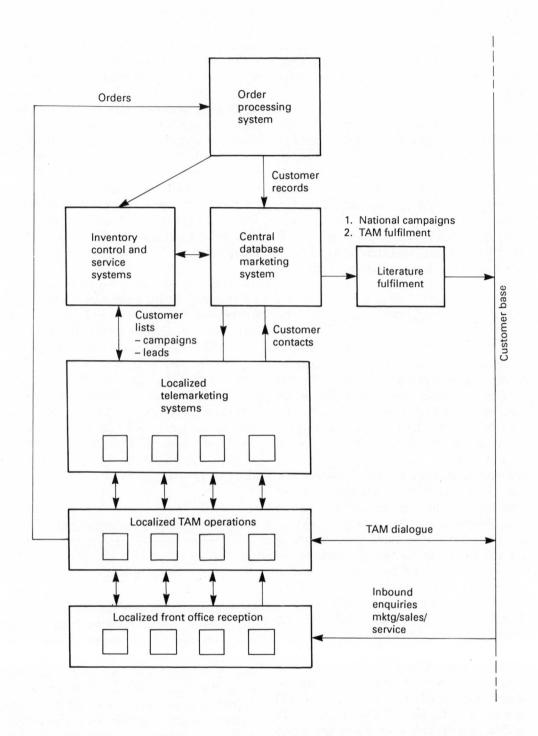

Figure 5.2 Linking the telemarketing system to other processing systems

any time. TAMs can also record their own conversations. They can then use these recordings to improve their technique. They therefore each need their own tape recorders as well as a turret (for dialling) and headset each.

Some TAM operations need a dedicated ACD or ACD emulation. Others can link into an existing ACD system (perhaps used in a general sales or service office). If the ACD facility or emulation is shared, the TAM operation will need a 'closed user group' facility, with sufficient outbound lines to allow all TAMs to call out simultaneously (i.e. at least one dedicated line per TAM position).

Lines

There should also be sufficient inbound capacity to support the TAMs' requirements. Here you are faced with the decision whether these lines should be Toll-free (in the USA) or Linklines (in the UK). We believe that if you can support the costs involved, you should do so. Whether your customers are private consumers or multinational businesses, you emit a very customer-oriented message by allowing the caller to call at your expense. It also acts as a strong incentive for you to make the best use of the call (and the customer's time while he is waiting to be answered or being answered). Because ordering these lines can take longer than ordinary lines, you should order them as soon as the location of your TAM office is known. It is suggested that at first you should provide a minimum of two inbound lines. This should suffice for up to about eight TAMs. Any more will require up to four lines. Beyond 16 TAMs, the number of lines increases further, but less than in proportion to the number of TAMs. Customer research and the ACD traffic statistics will tell you whether your customers feel they have to wait often for a free line, and if so, for how long.

If you are planning to increase the size of your TAM operation, do not forget to make provision for more inbound lines. Inbound call levels will be low to start with. But they will grow gradually, as you encourage customers to call. As long as these customer calls relate to sales (and not service) enquiries, they can be the cheapest way of selling and the best basis for building a strong relationship with customers. The only kind of service call that should be routinely dealt with by the customer's TAM is a complaint. This is because a well-handled complaint can build trust and loyalty and lead to more sales.

As well as telephones connected to the ACD, the TAM operation will need further telephones attached to your local switchboard. One of these should be in the TAM manager's office and the others in the support area, so make sure that you check the full requirement for telephone lines before ordering, whether direct exchange lines for connection to your ACD (at least one per TAM), or lines linking your ACD directly to your PBX. Remember to order Toll-free lines early.

Office equipment

Facsimile

Fax is essential as a medium in business-to-business communication, especially in any sales environment. Customers may ask for faxed confirmation of orders and of product specification. You may want the customer to fax information about their needs to you. If they are located on another site, your field sales staff will almost certainly request fax communication.

Photocopying

The TAM operation will probably need

immediate access to a photocopier. This is particularly likely for a paper-based approach, but even with an automated approach, many documents may need to be copied. You do not want your staff to waste valuable time looking for a working photocopier.

Computer-based systems

There are a number of standard and 'tailorable' computer systems that can be used to support a TAM operation. The most relevant benefits they can provide to a TAM operation are as follows:

- Provision of on-line scripts or call guides so that the TAMs are steered to cover all the required points in a structured way.
- Storing information about your customers and the dialogues you are having with them. This takes place as the TAMs are talking with the customers, and is especially effective if they are using call guides and matched contact records. The information can then be used either within the conversation, to trigger decisions about next steps, or in a future conversation, to enable the TAM to 'remember' customer details.
- As a diarying tool for customer callbacks within a sales cycle.
- To prompt fulfilment, either by providing a feed to an automatic literature fulfilment process, or even directly to a product distribution system, which in turn can be attached to a stock control system.

Relationship with the main database

Telemanagement must be based on a comprehensive database. This should

be borne in mind when choosing the system to support your operation. Some early implementers of TAM have supported TAM via a central database, on which they hold the company's entire customer information set, thus integrating the approach to the market. They have then used this database to feed information to local (smaller) telemarketing systems, which in turn have fed new information back into the central corporate database. Others have started out by using paper-based systems. Even if the main customer database is computerized, paper output has been taken from it for the TAM operation. This may sound strange, but it is not a bad idea. It ensures that the form of the feed from the main database is fully trialled before being programmed into a costly computer system for the TAMs.

Personal computer usage

As well as using the PCs as possible terminal emulators (linked to the telemarketing system), there are a number of applications which may be applicable to your operation. These include:

- processing pro-forma and customized letters to customers
- running spreadsheet analyses on past (and predicted) performance
- communicating with other parts of the organization via telex or electronic mail
- preparing standard (or tailored) quotations and contracts
- general word-processing applications

So far, our descriptions of the TAM operation has focused on rather technical factors. We now consider the most important element – the people in the TAM operation.

6

Staffing the TAM operation

Before recruiting can start, the responsibilities and roles of the TAMs, the TAM Operations Manager (see below) and the support staff must be assessed and specified. This specification includes writing full job descriptions for each post and producing a recruitment plan. In doing this, you should work as closely as possible with your sales and marketing functions as well as the personnel function.

Figure 6.1 is an example of a TAM organization chart. There are obviously other ways of arrangement. The critical point is to maintain the differentiation between the working team leader role (the TAM Operations Manager or TOM) and the more senior role of the TAM Sales Manager. The latter plans activities, ensures that the TAM operation has the right systems and support, and deals with the relationship of the TAM operation to the rest of the business. The operations manager must not be distracted by these issues, but must be left to get on with the job of managing a selling team.

The role of support staff is equally critical. Do not be tempted to economize

here. How many support staff you need depends on whether you are using a paper-based or automated system and on how liaison with the rest of your organization is handled. If you skimp on support, TAMs and the TOM will become overpaid clerical staff. They will not be doing enough selling or sales management – remember, these are what bring in the money! *Be warned — this is an easy mistake to make!*

A typical TAM organization will comprise a dedicated TAM Operations Manager, 8–10 TAMs (depending on the size of customer base to be managed) and a number of support staff (at the ratio of 1–1.5 support staff to 3 TAMs). The operations manager should ideally report to a sales manager who may well have related field sales people reporting to him or her as well as the TAM team. The main accountabilities of each member of the TAM operation are as follows:

- *TAM Sales Manager (TSM)* – Responsible for the strategic management of the operation, including initial set-up and integration into your national or local sales organization (depending on whether the TAM operation covers local or national sales).
- *TAM Operations manager (TOM)* – Responsible for operational management, in particular managing the TAMs, the support staff, and the

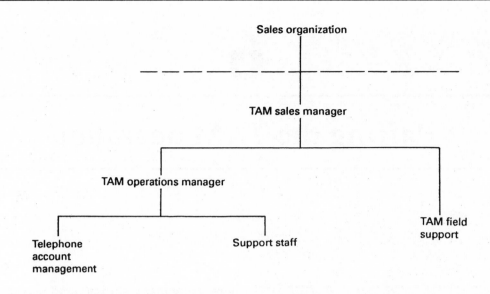

Figure 6.1 Suggested TAM organization

smooth running of the system.

- *Telephone Account Manager (TAMs)* – Responsible for managing the customer base, and for maximizing the sales of selected products and services.
- *Support staff* – Responsible for administering the various systems within the TAM operation. They allow managers time to manage and TAMs time to optimize phone usage.

Let us examine these roles in more detail.

TAM Sales Manager

The TAM Sales Manager (TSM) is responsible for:

- the strategic development of the TAM operation
- ensuring that the TAM operation is well integrated within the channel strategy of your company
- the medium-term development of staff within the TAM operation.

The strategic development of the operation involves its initial set up, its continual evolution, and the evolution of any product portfolios for which the TAM operation is an important sales channel. The TSM is also responsible for managing the TOM. The TSM should ensure that the TOM carries out the day-to-day operational work, and should allow the TSM to form a considered view as to how the TAM operation is performing, and how it should develop in the future.

TSMs should be fully responsible for staff assessment and counselling, as well as for training the TOM in counselling techniques. Do not assume that the TOM is an expert at this. You will need to ensure that TOMs are frequently coached and counselled in coaching and counselling their staff.

TSMs are also responsible for:

- campaign planning
- ensuring that information on the company's customer database is properly used by the TAM operation.

- interpreting all TAM results and measurements
- negotiating sales targets during start-up and development
- preventing panic sales or service campaigns which do not form part of long-term telemanaging objectives destroying the work of the TAM team

Throughout the evolution of the TAM operation (from conception to maturity) the TSM should integrate the operation within various local processes. To achieve a truly integrated approach, the TSM will need to liaise with the following:

- *Senior management* – To ensure their commitment and understanding, as well as to build TAM into the organization's channel strategy).
- *Marketing* – To develop TAM as an integrated sales channel, to co-ordinate any corporate marketing activity, and to provide feedback on the TAMs' experiences in selling your current products and services to your customers.
- *Various 'supply' channels* – To ensure that the products and services are available for your TAMs to sell.
- *Existing sales departments* – To ensure that no sales (or sales momentum) are lost due to a lack of internal communication.

The TSM has prime responsibility for choosing, measuring and motivating the staff within the TAM operation. The TSM should also work with the TOM (see below) to ensure that the maximum productivity is developed within the operation.

You may wish to combine the roles of TSM and TOM to save headcount. This could cause problems. The TOM should be completely focused on the 'nitty-gritty' of the TAM operation, while the TSM makes sure that the TAM operation works well with the rest of the company. If there is pressure on headcount, then the holder of the TSM post might have other sales responsibilities.

TAM Operations Manager

The TAM Operations Manager (TOM) should be responsible for the day-to-day running of the TAM operation.

This covers the following:

- Establishing and meeting TAM sales, revenue, productivity and activity targets, overall and for each TAM.
- Conducting regular skills evaluation reviews and coaching sessions with the TAMs by monitoring calls. This should take 30–50 per cent of the TOM's time.
- Acting as a 'surrogate customer' to ensure the continued provision of the highest quality customer service.
- Managing the personnel functions by recruiting, measuring and motivating subordinate staff.
- Controlling the effective use of any electronic systems (ACD, telemarketing system) in supporting the telephone operation.
- Generating periodic reports on sales, revenue and productivity for interpretation by the TSM.
- Managing the TAM operation's sales procedures by liaising with such departments as delivery, customer service, installation, and other sales departments. However, this time should be kept to a minimum – not more than 10 per cent of the TOM's time. It should always be logged.
- Managing the complete TAM process.

In addition to the above, TOMs should also be responsible for any campaign implementation, e.g. list cleaning and list management. Above all, the TOM should be in the telephone room, constantly supporting and tuning the operation and its people.

57

Telephone Account Manager

The Telephone Account Manager (TAM should work exclusively on the telephone and be responsible for managing and developing customers. However, TAMs should not be qualifiers and appointment setters. Their primary objective is to sell 'sight unseen' over the phone with the aid of promotional literature and demonstration facilities. You must avoid competition for customers or poaching between TAMs and field sales staff. This will confuse customers and increase selling costs. Any field salesperson should be used as a visiting specialist as agreed within your overall TAM strategy. In this strategy, field and office-based personnel share the same portfolio of products and services.

TAMS must be able to communicate the value of your services or products, identify applications/needs within their accounts and fulfil short-term and long-term needs. They must build a bond between their accounts and their own organizations, reinforcing corporate positioning, image and strategy.

Support staff

Support staff allow managers and TAMs to manage their own tasks productively and effectively. They should report directly to the TOM and be responsible for activities such as:

- sending out standard and customized letters
- sending out literature
- producing quotations
- completing contracts and sending them out to customers
- booking demonstrations
- gathering information from other departments at the TAMs' request
- ordering stationery

- creating spreadsheets and graphs on PCs
- processing and progressing any paper in the system (especially in a paper-based system)
- other general administration tasks.

Support staff are vital to the smooth running of the operation.

The TAM team

The TAM team needs to be one of the most tightly organized teams in your company. Teamwork is critical. TAMs work very closely with their office and field support staff and their management to achieve good sales results and to maintain the information needed to ensure a constantly high performance. For this reason your recruitment and training programme should place a very strong emphasis on team skills.

TAMs need the drive and discipline to 'carry on regardless' of the day-to-day problems. Being a TAM can be very frustrating. A succession of difficult or fruitless calls can be very demotivating. Try to minimize fruitless calling by better targeting. Nevertheless, there will still be hours or days when TAMs may feel that even the best support in the world will not help. Confidence and enthusiasm under duress are therefore critical factors to look for during recruitment.

Telemanaging disciplines are very different from many sales jobs. There is a clear routine to each day, to which TAMs need to become accustomed. They are – in the best sense of the phrase – part of a very powerful sales machine. This machine works only because each part of it works – smoothly and on time. This even applies to the timing of tea and coffee breaks. The level of detail required should be clearly specified in their job description and tested thoroughly during recruitment.

Coaching

For the TAM operation to succeed, much on-the-job coaching is needed for TAMs and support staff. This is in addition to formal training, which provides the basic marketing and sales skills and product knowledge. Coaching must reinforce and further develop technique and team skills. It must also cover company sales procedures – especially the informal 'network' which in many companies actually makes things happen. The TAM Operations Manager (TOM) will be kept very busy, particularly in the early months after start-up, administering the TAM process, and will need some support in this area during these early days of running the operation.

The TOM should be the TAMs' coach. The TSM's responsibility extends, of course, to the coaching requirements of the TOM. Effective coaching is needed here, especially during the start-up period. This 'cascade' approach to coaching ensures the building of a strong team. It also ensures that each person in the TAM team understands the role of the rest of the team members. We have seen it work well. We have also seen the poor performance that results when it is lacking.

Line management in practice

The TOM is the line manager of the TAM operation. As an intensely sales-oriented operation, the TAM operation should be run on a regular weekly and monthly cycle.

The monthly cycle is mainly a reporting cycle. At the end of each month, performance reports should be prepared and circulated to senior sales management. The latter may wish to compare the sales and costs figures for the TAM operation with those for field sales and other sales channels. The monthly figures are likely to reveal any significant problems or opportunities developing. Performance by product will be reviewed, as will the performance of different call guides (perhaps via tests). The month end (and perhaps the quarter end) are likely to be important times for bonus calculations and motivational awards (e.g. the top performing 'club').

To the average TAM, however, the weekly cycle will be the one that keeps the focus on achievement and provides the framework for evaluation, training and coaching. Unless time is set aside for these activities every week (and in some cases every day) they will not happen often enough. Morale will begin to suffer. Time management is central to telemanagement – for the TOM it is crucial. Unless the TOM sets enough time aside for these activities, the TAMs' need for the constant encouragement and motivation provided through evaluation, training and coaching will not be met.

Daily routine

At the start of every day, there should be a brief meeting led by the TOM. It should cover immediate issues, updating on performance so far, resolve any pressing problems, review performance and provide motivation. You may want to have a similar but shorter meeting immediately after lunch, picking up any issues raised in the morning and continuing to motivate.

During the day, the operations manager should keep a check on the state of the filing system, the activities of support staff, and the quality of dialogue being achieved with customers. ACD statistics should be checked to ensure that all TAMs are meeting their set productivity standards. Towards the end of the day, the various reports produced by the computer or support staff should be reviewed. If the system is properly computerized, these reports will be available at the end of each working day, so can be studied then. Any issues arising in them can then be addressed in the following morning meeting.

At the end of each week, a meeting of all operational staff should be held. This should not be a rushed meeting. Your staff will have worked very hard all week. They will need to break to consider what they have achieved over the week, and review the work with others. This meeting should include presentations from TAMs on subjects such as what they have learnt during the week, problem solution, and successes. Team-building activities could also be scheduled here. Use the time to allow TAMs to reflect on achievements and experiences and to allow the whole team to review performance. This will build a sense of responsibility and a feeling of achievement, closing the week's work on a strongly positive note.

At the end of each week, the TAMs should be asked what goals they will be setting themselves for the following week. Reports of the week so far should be reviewed to identify opportunities as a prelude to this goal setting. The aim should be to ensure that each TAM starts the week with good memories and keen to hit a new personal target.

The importance of process

However you run your day, week, or month, the importance of training, communication, motivation and structure cannot be overemphasized. A well-run TAM operation needs to be maintained to keep it running well. This means people maintenance, not system maintenance. Keep the way that you do this under review, both in your own

mind and in open discussion with your TAMs. They are the ones who work with the customers, and they are likely to have many good ideas about how your management process can help them do it better.

The recruitment process

The recruitment process is a continuing part of the TAM operation's job. This is because you must expect some staff turnover in what is a very demanding job. Recruitment should therefore be built into the routine of the TAM operation. It should not be considered as a special exercise. The costs of having a TAM position vacant are high. If a position is vacant, the systems, support staff, management and facilities costs are still there, but the revenue will fall. Worse – customers to whom we have promised a high-quality, customer-oriented relationship will find they are neglected. A good TOM will be in such close touch with TAMs that the likelihood of staff leaving will be identified well in advance and the required recruitment activity planned.

You may wish (or be forced) to use *temporary TAMs*. This is not impossible, but the costs of training a TAM are so high, and the value of experience so great that it would take an assignment of many months to justify the use of temporary staff. If you are forced to do this, then you would be advised to develop a special relationship with an employment agency, so that you can quickly identify the kind of staff required. If fact, a much stronger proposition may be to have an internal reserve team who have been part-trained. You can do this by recruiting 'reserve' TAMs as TAM support staff. This gives career development within the team (always good for morale) and reduces problems of using inexperienced new staff. Support staff know the dynamics of the TAM job and all the operational systems. These constitute 30 per cent of training.

Where to start

The non-routine part of recruitment consists of what you have to do before you recruit any TAMs at all – this requires clarifying the role of TAMs. You also need to work closely with your personnel department to identify how your company's recruitment procedures should be adapted to the needs of a TAM operation. Then you should prepare job descriptions for all posts in the TAM operation, working with the Sales/ Marketing and Personnel functions.

Management and support staff should be recruited according to your normal company recruitment procedures. These staff need to be of quite high calibre. They are required to get a new operation going and manage it effectively. The TOM also requires significant sales and/or sales management experience. Telemarketing experience helps. This is one reason for recruiting managers from outside.

TAMs can come from within the organization or from outside. Internal or external advertising should be carefully planned, taking into account the typical lead times for advertisement placement, interviewing, job offering and acceptance. Some characteristics of the TAM – apart from those related to the industry or nature of the service or product they are having to sell – are listed below.

TAM profile

TAMs must

- be 'natural communicators'
- be able to relate to all levels of

seniority of customer staff, be a good conversation opener and a firm closer
- be capable of selling commodities, concepts and value-added
- be self-motivated yet amenable to motivation and management
- be team players who shoulder responsibility for concluding their own work
- possess the emotional stability to withstand frustration and rejection, combined with the stamina and commitment to manage volume calling and accomplish targets
- be able to work in a structured, logical manner
- possess acute listening skills, and be decisive, persuasive and persistent
- be able to identify and resolve objections, and convey warmth and confidence

Finally, don't forget a sense of fun – a TAM, after all, should be able to keep customers happy!

TAM experience

To have sales or account management experience (either telephone-based or face-to-face) is desirable. Telesales experience is not necessarily valuable – it depends on the complexity and objectives of the applicant's teleselling role. The applicant should have some experience related to the product/ services you sell. In some cases this may be a prerequisite to starting the job; in others a lack of relevant experience can be overcome during training and subsequently on the job. The approach you take is partly determined by the quality of your internal recruitment pool.

Recruitment steps

The recruitment process should include the following steps:

Advertise

This should be conducted according to normal practices within your organization. Recruiting can be achieved using recruitment agencies or you may want to advertise directly yourself. The advertisement should direct applicants to telephone a specific number that is dedicated to this purpose. It must be made as easy as possible for the applicants to get through. It is recommended that the internal and external advertising be conducted simultaneously. The same procedure should be adopted thereafter, however, for both streams.

Initial screening

Whoever does your initial screening, either the Project Manager or your Personnel Department must be fully briefed about the TAM job and be comfortable with qualifying initial applicants and information-seekers over the phone. They should be armed with a job description and be able to record the number of applicants from each advertisement and to quantify the success/failure rate at initial screening.

The screening should cover:

- *Educational qualifications* – does the applicant meet the basic requirements for the grade your company has accorded the job?
- *Internal applicants* – are they suitably qualified for the grade, using your company's normal criteria?
- *Experience* – does the applicant have the experience you are seeking, particularly having sold on the phone? If not (e.g. non-sales phone experience), assess their understanding of the role and capabilities at a basic level by exploring their sales and communications potential.
- *Telephone manner* – at a very basic level, does the applicant possess the communications skills essential to the job?

If the applicant fails to meet any of these criteria, then he or she will not be able to succeed as a TAM and there is no point in going any further. The candidate should ideally be told immediately over the phone and this should be confirmed as soon as possible by letter.

Successful applicants at this stage should be made aware that:

- they will have to participate in a further telescreen interview of approximately 20 minutes
- this telephone interview will include a role play
- they should find a private area from which to make the call for this interview
- this call will be scheduled for a definite time – normally one which will not inconvenience them in their existing job (e.g. lunchtime, evening or weekend); at this time, they must call a specified number which will test their punctuality

If they are successful at this stage, they will then have a further face-to-face interview before they may be offered the job.

Telescreen (telephone interview)

To recruit TAMs successfully, a formal interview should be conducted over the telephone before any face-to-face meeting. Your customers will not normally meet your TAMs face-to-face. It is important to understand the impression they make under pressure, using the phone as the medium. This also avoids the risk of prejudgement because of appearances (whether good or bad).

The telescreen is crucial for the following reasons:

- It gives you an opportunity to assess how good the applicants are at communicating and selling themselves in a short space of time over the telephone. *This after all is what they will be asked to do if they are successful.*
- It gives you the chance to experience at first hand what it is like to make the same call to many different 'customers'. It also shows you the advantages of using a call guide in a structured way. This experience should prove invaluable in later coaching sessions with the TAMs.

A call guide for the telescreen process should be prepared prior to the process starting. This is because, with possibly many tens of interviews to conduct, a high degree of uniformity is required so that the different applicants can be fairly assessed. A formal system of scoring each applicant should also be applied to help minimize any subjectivity and to provide a consistent approach.

The telescreen interview should, where possible, be taped for later playback either prior to the face-to-face interview or if you want a colleague to help you decide. To telescreen, you need to be in a quiet closed room. You may find it easier to invite the candidates in to your location (or an hotel) to conduct the telescreen in a more controlled manner.

Paper sift

Applicants who are successful at the telescreen stage should then receive a documentation pack containing paperwork such as the application form, a health declaration, and a job description. When all the paperwork has been returned by the applicants who wish to proceed, a paper sift should be conducted to narrow down the field further.

Personality profiling

You may want a personality profile review. Such psychometric tests have been used by many companies and could be useful with TAM recruitment, where people with the right temperament are needed to do a good job. Several companies offer profiling services and your personnel group may help you find a suitable one. This is a specialist skill – do not try to devise your own system.

Face-to-face interviews

These interviews should be scheduled with all applicants who pass the telescreen, to last for about one hour and be conducted by operational and personnel staff jointly. Information derived from the telescreen and any personality profiling should be included in the interview for further development. Questions should focus on the applicant's understanding of the job and of the concept of TAM. Do not oversell TAM. Be alert for reasons why people might not make good TAMs or team members. Faulty recruitment is costly. A this stage applicants should be evaluated for their fit within the TAM team as a whole, as well as individually.

Final selections

As noted earlier, final selections should take into account all the data accumulated during the complete recruitment process. If necessary, use the tapes of the telescreen to review the applicant's strengths and weaknesses. The telescreen and the face-to-face interviews will be most significant. Any personality profile should be used to back up areas of uncertainty from these interviews, if relevant.

At every stage all applicants (successful and unsuccessful) should be notified as soon as possible of the outcome of their various interviews. Applicants who are selected as TAMs at final selection should be offered a job according to the accepted procedures adopted by your organization.

All TAMs and the TOM should be told of any mandatory attendance on training courses at job-offer stage. It helps if dates for these are already set and can be booked with recruits immediately – to prevent holiday clashes, for example.

Sample call guide for telescreening interview

Use this to develop your own guide.

Description of post:................................

Purpose of call guide:.............................

*Good morning/afternoon. This is ....
Thank you for calling. Please let me explain the purpose of this telephone interview. I would like to see how you can communicate over the telephone so that I can determine whether you are appropriate for the job of .... which you have applied for. The interview will take about 20 minutes. During this time I shall ask you a few questions about yourself and your experience. I shall also tell you something about the job. You may then want to ask me some questions.*

You may wish to include a small role play in the interview, basing it on the type of customer and product you are dealing with, and the role you are planning for TAMs. If so then you should prepare the applicant by telling them that this is what you plan to do. Thereafter, structure your interview to include the following information about them:

Personal: *name; address; age; sex; marital status, etc.*
Current job: *position; company; responsibilities; goals; performance; salary*

Experience (current and previous): *selling; telephone; account management; working to targets; degree of supervision; if tele-selling – use of scripting, use of systems, applications, use of call recording procedures; training*
Motivation: *reasons for leaving; why this new job; why last job*

Tell them about the job. Ask them whether they have any questions for you. Explain the process of interviews, etc. from this stage onwards, and say someone will be in touch with them soon.

An example of a scoring sheet for evaluating a telescreened candidate is shown in Figure 6.2

Training

A thorough training programme should be developed for all members of the TAM team. This training should include the initial product and skills training required before the team can start operating, the on-going coaching and counselling needed each and every day, and refresher training to concentrate on new skills, new products and re-visiting existing skills and products.

A suggested series of courses is shown below.

TAM manager training

Set up training

This is to include:

- TAM principles
- how TAM is to be used in your organization
- staff, system, accommodation requirements

TAM telescreen interview

Mark each applicant on a separate sheet and compare resultant scores together with any added view

Interviewer name:_____

Applicant name: _____

Date:_____ Time: _____ Duration: _____

Comments:_____

_____

_____

1. *Selling skills*	*Score 1–10*	(1 = bad, 10 = excellent)

Opening...................................._____

Closing...................................._____

Objection handling........................._____

Questioning................................._____

Benefits...................................._____

2. *Communications skills*	*Score 1–20*	(1 = bad, 20 = excellent)

Listening...................................._____

Understanding................................_____

Clarity....................................._____

Responsiveness..............................._____

Pace......................................._____

Explaining..................................._____

3. *Relevant experience*	*Score 1–5*	(1 = bad, 5 = excellent)

Selling....................................._____

Telephone..................................._____

Office-based................................._____

Your industry..............................._____

Account management.........................._____

Total score: _____

Figure 6.2 Sample score sheet for TAM telescreen interview

- project planning principles

This training is likely to take at least a week. Without running a pilot, you will find it difficult to develop the material for this course. If your company is small, with only one TAM manager to be trained, this training is likely to be provided by the external consultants retained to help you establish TAM, or even yourself! If your company is large, with several medium-sized or one large TAM operation planned, then a single team pilot will provide the material to train all the TAM managers.

Operational training

This is to include:

- TAM operational procedures
- TAM management procedures
- coaching and counselling skills

This training is likely to take at least a week. The operational procedures may have been derived from external experience, or else worked out from first principles. If you have limited information to go on, you may wish to treat training as a hybrid of training and procedure development.

For both kinds of training, we believe that you must maintain a very low trainee:trainer ratio, as low as 2:1 or even 1:1. This is because it is absolutely critical that trainees are ready to set up and run their operations as soon as they have completed their training. The two periods of training should be separated by a few weeks, during which the TAM manager starts the process for setting up the operation.

TAM support training

This is to include:

- TAM operational procedures
- limited product training
- TAM administrative procedures

This training is likely to take about a week, depending upon the complexity of the operation procedures, and whether you are starting with a paper-based or computerized system. The contents of this course will be the details of the operational procedures, the

management aspects of which will have been trained into the operations manager.

TAM training

This is to include:

- TAM principles
- TAM operational procedures
- product training
- using the telephone
- selling skills
- using scripts/call guides

TAMs need to understand the principles of telemanaging customers, covered in Chapters 1 and 2. They also need to understand the operational and administrative procedures (their version of what the support people receive). Most important of all, they must have product training. We believe that you will need to allow at least two weeks of basic training before the product training. The length of the latter depends upon the breadth and technical complexity of the product range you will be marketing through TAM.

You should intersperse product training with the introduction of call guides/ scripts on those products and with lots of role-playing between TAMs, using call guides. This will consolidate their skills and product understanding.

Introducing TAM

So far the people, processes, systems, support and facilities required to make TAM work have been described. We now need to examine how to make all the required changes in your organization.

7

The project plan

Introducing TAM into any organization is an exacting process. Setting up a TAM operation itself could take many months, from the start of the approval cycle to the first live customer call. If your company is setting up several TAM operations, going live at different times, it might take two or three years until all operations are live.

As we saw in Chapters 5 and 6, setting up a TAM operation involves many tasks, as follows:

- *Accommodation* – Suitable accommodation has to be found. This in turn has to be converted (if necessary); re-furbished; and furnished; fitted out with the requisite power, lighting and heating.
- *TAM systems* – The systems have to be specified, chosen, installed and tested. The telephony has to be specified, chosen, installed and tested.
- *Staff* – The staff have to be specified, recruited, brought on board and trained.
- *Support systems and processes* – The support systems, including databases, fulfilment arrangements and the tracking and call-back processes, have to be designed, delivered and installed. Some of these may well be paper-based to start with. Note that the TAM operation may want to store information about customers that is too detailed to be stored on the main database, e.g. the personal situation of decision makers, consideration or usage of competitive products, and TAM contact cycle details.
- *Management systems and processes* – Management systems (paper-based or computerized) have to be designed and put in place. Measurements must be designed and processes defined.
- *Portfolio/product/customer targeting* – From decisions about general customer groups to be targeted, detailed customer lists must be generated and assigned to individual TAMs. Products must be selected (ideally every one of your products that target customers could use) and stocks checked. Call guides need to be written and tested with experienced sales managers and through market research.

Many different groups of people will be involved. They include your facilities people, systems and telecommunications staff, marketing and sales people, finance and general management. These all work to different disciplines and need to be educated as to what TAM is, how it works and what its objectives are. They all need to understand why the TAM operation must be set up in a specific way.

Because TAM is an important programme, and because the requirements are highly specific, we suggest that a project planning approach be used for implementing TAM. This will help you particularly in the following areas:

- It will ensure that what is asked of the team is actually achievable.
- It should ensure that activities are started (and hopefully finished) on time.
- It should allow different departments and senior managers to view (and review) what their activities are and when they are scheduled to start and finish.
- It allows you to see the affect of changes (slippages etc.) on the whole project.
- It gives you a framework for reviewing progress.

The project planning model

To help you manage this process, we have developed a model of how to implement a single TAM operation. You may wish to use project management software to check that this model is totally consistent and does not stretch your resources unduly. Any standard microcomputer project management software should be sufficient. We believe that this sort of project will need to be managed by a combination of computer software and paper-based variations, using the computer output. This is because many people involved in the project may not have access to your model. Also, unless there is a reasonable degree of proficiency in using project management software in your company, much time may be wasted in getting to grips with the software.

One way of proceeding is to develop a template using software, and use this as the ideal from which departures are made, using paper-based plans. However, the advantage of staying with the software is that it will enable you to view a project in many different ways. Most importantly it will enable you to:

- sort out diaried events
- apportion responsibilities for parts of the project sensibly and fairly
- identify changes necessitated as a result of any slippages
- identify when there is potential conflict over the use of key resources – in particular when *you* are due to be in another place at the same time

Thus, if the key protagonists in making the TAM operation happen to have access to, and experience of, project management software, then you should use it. In the description below, we have identified the 25 critical steps. There are of course far more in practice. One of your tasks should be to develop these further to suit your requirements, as you progress towards setting up your TAM operation. Figure 7.1 gives an overview of the process. The following describes each task in the plan.

1. *Business Plan prepared*
The time taken to create and approve a business plan depends on your organization's decision processes. The main purpose of including it in the Project Plan is to show that it needs to be allowed for in your planning process. Even if the creation of TAM was foreshadowed or planned in detail in your company-wide business or marketing plan, this may have been at a general level. The TAM Business Plan may be a much more detailed document, indicating precisely the resource requirements, timetables and likely results. TAM may be a big investment for you. You must be able to show how much money will be spent, when and with what return.
2. *Business Plan approved*
The Business Plan should be approved by your senior management, and any functional heads, such as Personnel and

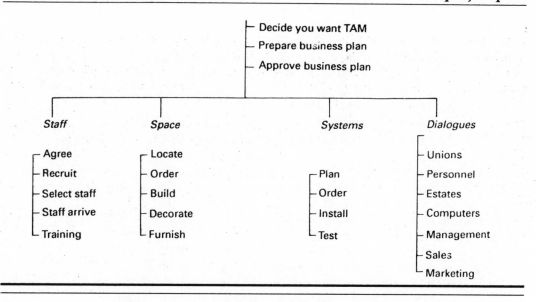

Figure 7.1 Overview of project plan

Sales, who will be involved or affected either by the setting up (e.g. Personnel) or by the running (e.g. Sales) of the TAM team. These people need to commit *their* resources right from the beginning.

3. *Implementation manager recruited*

This covers the recruitment of the TAM Implementation Manager. In many organizations this will be the TAM Sales Manager (TSM). Chapter 6 which discusses staff gives further details on the role and responsibilities of the TSM.

4. *Check point 1*

The first check point covers the approval of the business plan and the commitment to the plan prior to implementation. It signals the last point before serious commitments of resource start to take place.

5. *Arrange implementation team*

The first task of the TAM Implementation Manager (TIM) is to set up an implementation team within the organization. This team should include managers of the relevant groups involved in the set-up of the TAM operation. The TIM may or may not have a role in running the TAM operation. We believe that it should probably be a senior sales manager who is likely to have the TAM operation within his direct line of

command. If the TIM is too junior, he or she will not be able to marshal the resources of your company, nor be able to capture its attention and imagination, to the required extent.

The members of your team are likely to include:

● senior management (their support will be needed continually throughout the project)
● estates
● personnel
● data processing (for computers and data communications)
● telecommunications (for telephony and telecommunications)
● field sales force and sales office
● marketing (for campaign-related activities and co-ordination with other marketing functions)
● product management and delivery
● operations managers (manufacturing, service operations)

6. *TAM Operations Manager (TOM) recruited*

The TAM Operations Manager is a critical member of the TAM team. We

69

suggest that the TOM be recruited as early as possible to help with the set-up process and to get involved with the TAM operation well before it goes live. If possible, the TOM should be recruited before other members of the TAM team are recruited (the TAMs themselves and TAM support staff).

7. *Accommodation secured*

The most important physical requirement for the TAM operation is the accommodation needed to house it. Which accommodation is chosen will depend on what is available. For example, you may have to look for new accommodation if there is no space available within existing premises. Resist the temptation to use basements! They are inherently depressing places, however much you invest in them.

8. *Staff recruited*

It is important to start the recruitment process as soon as possible. Involve your Personnel function. Pay equal attention to recruiting the TAMs and the TAM support staff.

The TAM job is a unique one, and a special recruiting process has been designed for it. As shown in Chapter 6, this process involves a telescreening (interview over the telephone), a face-to-face interview and a personal profile questionnaire.

The TAM support staff also play an important role in making up the TAM team. The recruitment process adopted here should encourage you to look within your own organization wherever possible. This helps generate within the organization much-needed commitment to and enthusiasm for TAM.

9. *Systems ordered*

Telephony, computer and communications requirements of the TAM operation are covered in Chapter 5. In agreeing requirements, you should involve the experts from your organization. They should be able to guide and advise you in this task. It is also important to get them involved and supportive of the TAM plans. This should help ensure that the installation of the various computer and communication systems is achieved smoothly and on time.

10. *Furniture ordered*

All office furniture, including workstations, filing cabinets, chairs and waste-paper bins, should be ordered in good time. This ensures that they are ready before the 'go live' date. Any other furniture and office fixtures and fittings and all office stationery should also be ordered well in advance.

11. *Check point 2*

The second check point for the TAM Implementation Team is scheduled to check that there have been no problems or omissions during the ordering stage. It also checks that all parties are set to deliver their portion of the project satisfactorily and on time. It is a critical check point. Before this point, the major investment has been of management resource. Items which have been ordered could in principle be cancelled. Beyond this point, money is being spent in earnest, and the commitment is made not to cancel equipment ordered.

12. *Setting up the access to relevant database*

This involves ensuring that the database(s) or lists, that are going to be used to generate the names that the TAMs are going to call, are actually set up ready to produce these names. This may be a paper list production for each TAM, or may be an electronic link to your customer database. In either case you should ensure that names are allocated to each TAM and that a mechanism for feeding back marketing information to the database is set up and ready. You should also generate some test lists, to ensure that the process moves smoothly and that the data are good.

13. *Setting up fulfilment procedures*

It is important to ensure that both literature and product/service fulfilment procedures are set up and ready. In the case of literature fulfilment, an estimate should be made of the amount of the various pieces, and a supply ordered accordingly. This is also the time to design formats and procedures to enable standard letters, proposals, quotations and contracts to be easily and readily produced.

14. *Build/fit/furnish*

This task covers building the various walls and offices required for the TAM operation, as well as re-furbishing and decorating the accommodation to the required standards. It should also include the installation of all power supplies and lighting. A flexible wiring system makes it easy to reorganize to give variety and to allow extra equipment to be installed later – particularly important if you are starting paper-based and expect to computerize later while the TAM operation stays live.

Also included here is the installation of all the furniture ordered above. Attention to detail is required. Items of furniture, such as desks and filing cabinets, are easy to remember, but do not forget minor items, such as filing trays and (very big!) waste paper bins.

15. *Accommodation ready*

This check point requires that all the accommodation, furnishings, fittings and facilities be completed satisfactorily by the required date. It is a prerequisite to installing the computers, telephony and communications lines. Note that provision for these installations should have been made when considering the design and re-furbishing of the accommodation.

16. *Check point 3*

The third check point for the TAM Implementation Team is designed to fall immediately after the accommodation has become available. At this check point, a review is conducted to assess the feasibility of continuing to work to the proposed 'go live' date.

17. *Systems installed*

Systems installed refers to the installation of the computers, telephony and communications lines. All systems must be installed and ready for the systems test prior to the ultimate check point (Check Point 4).

18. *Systems tested*

At this stage all the electronic and electrical systems are tested. This includes all computers, telephony (including the ACD), communications lines (including toll free), and the electrical power supplies and lighting. The tests should be complete commissioning tests, with all systems tested as they will be used in live-running conditions. Take particular note of screen refresh/response times if you are using an automated telemarketing system. You must simulate this under full, all-system-loaded, operating conditions. A slow system is the death of telemarketing, and is far more difficult to use than a paper system.

19. *Stationery in place*

The various paper-based facilities and lists should be ready by this stage. They include: stationery, literature, letters, price lists, calling lists and call guides.

20. *Check point 4*

The fourth Check point is designed to ensure that the TAM operation is completely ready to be used in a fully live situation. If it is not completely ready at this stage then the 'go live' date may be changed to accommodate the delay. This could affect the staffing of the operation as the TAMs and support staff will be scheduled to arrive soon after this check point.

21. *Management training*

You need a training workshop for the TSM and TOM, to ensure that they are completely familiar with the operational procedures and systems for the TAM operation. It should also cover the skills elements of managing, leading, coaching, counselling and motivating the TAM team.

22. *Support staff training*

Support staff will be trained separately in the operational procedures and the support system necessary to run the TAM operation.

23. *TAM training*

This training will cover the TAM

process, product details (features, advantages, benefits), sales and communications skills, and using the various TAM systems and aids.

24. *Lists ready*
All the calling lists (whether paper or electronic) should be ready for the TAMs to start calling. This means they must be loaded onto the system or waiting in each TAM's filing system.

25. *Live calls*
By this stage the whole TAM operation is ready to 'go live'. The TAMs start calling real customers from their lists. The business of Telephone Account Management commences. The TOM will need to stop and coach each TAM several times a day in the early weeks of calling, to build skills and confidence.

It is when live calls begin that the support that you provide for the TAMs is most severely tested. The next chapter shows you how to prepare the right support for your TAMs.

8

Support and management

Support

Support is needed:

- to provide the TAMs with the right customer names at the right time for pro-active, outbound calling
- to keep this calling process going for each customer, until the call cycle is finished (i.e. until the customer has either bought or not bought, and the cycle is terminated until the next cycle is started)
- to allow literature and product/ service fulfilment to happen as a result of the dialogue with the customer during the calling cycle

Databases

For telemanagement to work, your approach to outbound telephone calls must be co-ordinated with other marketing and selling activities. One way of ensuring that this co-ordination takes place is through the database of customers that you use for TAM calling.

If your company uses a customer database for implementing other communications with customers, the TAM database should be co-ordinated with it. However, when you start with TAM, you may not want to invest in developing a new database. You may even be unwilling to spend on adapting your existing database for the TAM operation. If so, you can use your main database to provide the names and basic details required to start the calling cycle and keep it going. In this case, the TAM operation will be treated as a series of direct marketing campaigns. Selecting for these campaigns and entering the results of them on the database can be done as for any other campaign. If you are piloting TAM, and not sure whether it will succeed for your company or for a particular group of customers, then this approach may be the best.

If your company is large, your customer marketing database may be very large. It may be used not only for direct marketing but also for sales force support and marketing planning. If you have this kind of database, there may be additional problems in using it to support the TAM operation. For example, your national database may be designed for batch processing. It may involve carefully designed selections being extracted and tested, and responses entered back onto the system later on. It may be able to contain only a limited amount of data about each customer. If it is used for marketing and sales force planning, its prime role may be to carry out counts of populations with different characteristics or lists of people with those characteristics; or it may be actively product, revenue or geographically based if its main use is for basic sales reporting and/or prospecting.

Ideally, the TAM database should be accessible on-line. This is not essential, however, as it is possible to run a TAM operation with a system working in batch mode. This would require changes in customer details to be entered later. If this is done overnight, it will only cause problems for relationships where there is often more than one contact per day with a given customer.

As system capabilities evolve, on-line processing of large databases is likely to become easier. Problems of consistency between your main database and the TAM database are likely to fade. In the interim, hybrid solutions may be used, such as maintaining on-line processing capability only for certain customers at any one time (e.g. those selected as targets for a particular campaign).

When you initiate your TAM operation, you may find it easier to arrange for customer data extractions to be made from the main database, and your data to be added back in batch mode. Your own TAM database should be designed to meet the needs of the TAM operation. It should not be heavily compromised by the needs of the main database. The only concession to your main database is that the customer files should be compatible and keyed by the same variables.

Once the TAM operation is running properly, and on a permanent basis, you will need further systems work done. This is because a campaign-oriented database may not be ideal for the TAM operation. For example, most campaign-oriented databases do not allow scheduling of individual customer contacts. Also, TAM databases tend to cover

fewer customers in much greater detail than general customer marketing databases, because the latter usually cover prospects and very infrequent users as well as core users. TAM databases focus on active customers.

Once your database (TAM database or TAM section of your main database) is designed or redesigned to meet the TAM operation's needs, it becomes your main basis for:

- generating names for the next calling cycle
- tracking progress and planning calls within a current cycle

Calling cycles may be on a fixed period basis. For example, all customers might be called every three months, or you may do it on an individual customer basis. In this case, customers are called depending on their particular needs. Some may therefore be called every six weeks and others every six months. Yet others might want to schedule each calling interval individually.

After one calling cycle, the database starts to yield useful information. After two or three calling cycles, you should have accumulated enough data on customers to help you develop a really deep understanding of your market. The picture you build up will include:

- product requirements
- use profiles (your products and competitors')
- customer profiles
- buying processes, including decision-making unit composition
- responsiveness to communication

This information should become the life blood of your marketing department and represents a unique asset to your organization, and should be used to drive product development as well as marketing and sales campaign development across a range of media, with the

TAM relationship as the focal point for personalization and sales closing.

Only *you* have this information. It should allow you to satisfy the needs of your customers better. Your relationship with them will improve. This will make them better customers. They will be more satisfied with your products and services. They will be more impressed by your company.

Database contents

If your customers are business customers, where possible your TAM database should hold the following information on them:

- names of contacts (decision makers) – possibly several in each company.
- title
- position of contact in company
- name of business
- business address
- telephone number of contact
- telephone number of main business (if different)
- type of business (industry code etc.)
- products/services (yours) already purchased (number, model, value)
- salesperson responsible (this should become the TAM)
- responses to past campaigns, including recency and frequency of responses and purchases
- decision-making authorities
- business needs
- size of company (turnover, number of employees)
- relationship with other companies (parent, subsidiary)
- competitors' products/services (number, model, maker, value)
- due-to-buy information
- budgetary details (amounts, financial year data)
- history of the TAM calling cycle (call backs scheduled etc.)
- results of the TAM calling cycle (sale/ no sale; attendance at demonstra-

tion, exhibition; literature sent; contract sent etc.)
- if sale, then number, model, value, date of installation/commencement of service

Use of the database

The database is used in four separate ways:

1 As a source of customer names for pro-active account management calls.
2 As a means of controlling the calling cycle for each customer.
3 As a source of increasingly accurate and relevent information about customers and their needs, to help you sell to them and bring to the market products which meet their needs better.
4 As a source of information to support individual account development planning, overall marketing planning and revenue targeting.

The combination of all four is essential for telemanagement to work.

TAM call strategy

As we stressed in Chapter 4, the call strategy applied in the TAM process has to relate to the primary tasks of the TAM. These are to cover the customer base pro-actively and to increase the revenue by selling your products and services to the customer, based on your understanding of needs in relation to those products. The results of all calls must be accurately recorded for the process to work. These include all the possible types of call the TAM may be involved in, namely:

- outbound from the database/list
- outbound call-backs during the sales cycle

- outbound as a result of leads passed to the TAM from inbound enquiries from other sources
- account-managed customer calls direct to the TAM

Properly planned and managed support is critical for the smooth running of a TAM operation. At each stage the next activity, often dependent on the outcome of the current activity, should have been determined in advance. This is the TAM contact strategy. This process is taken to its most detailed level in the generation of call guides.

Call guides

The structure and content of the call guide should be entirely determined by the overall call strategy. Suppose that the call strategy in a particular call cycle is to sell product X. Then the call guide should be totally focused on establishing which customers are suspects for X, qualifying them into prospects, and finally converting them to a sale. However, this should be done in a way that is consistent with the overall TAM relationship and strategy. This in turn consists of a series of cycles – while we are selling one product, we have our eye on the next! The process must be flexible enough to enable the TAM to take advantage of unexpected opportunities to sell other products that arise in discussions with the customer.

Call strategy and the customer relationship

By having a series of related steps that conform to an overall strategy the TAM begins to build up a pro-active (and predetermined) business relationship with the customer. This relationship exists for the satisfaction (better, more focused support, service and solutions) of the customer. But it must also support the profit (more products/services sold to happier customers) of your organization. Without the right support, none of this will be possible.

TAM differs from other telemarketing functions in many respects. The most important is that the TAMs themselves are responsible for the complete process, up to and including closing the sale. The call strategy may well result in a sale (the most obvious conclusion). But it must take into account the fact that the customer may not want to purchase immediately. The call strategy must therefore include a call-back option to keep the dialogue going. This continuous calling of the customer base, in a controlled way, is the essence of TAM, and only made possible through provision of comprehensive support to the TAMs, so that they can focus on managing the relationship with the customer. Indeed, the key advantage of telemanaging is the control it gives your company in developing your market, while at the same time making the customer feel in control.

Action and fulfilment

Many actions are triggered in the TAM operation as a result of TAMs calling their customers. Where possible, these actions should be carried out by the support group within the TAM operation. Sometimes, however, the actions will require someone from outside the operation to carry them out.

Examples of follow-up actions carried out within the operation are:

- sending out literature, price lists etc.
- preparing and sending out letters
- preparing and sending out quotations

- preparing and sending out contracts
- passing on leads to others in your company
- arranging for sales visits, product demonstrations
- passing on signed contracts to delivery and billing units

Examples of actions implemented outside the TAM operation include:

- using a literature fulfilment house for bulk, standard literature fulfilment
- field sales visits
- product demonstrations
- processing signed contracts (unless this is done by TAM support staff)
- fulfilling orders (e.g. installing, delivering, or posting products, providing services)
- field service and customer care visits

To make sure that all the above actions are capable of being carried out, the whole TAM process needs to be fully specified, from the time the customer is first called, to the end of any of the above outcomes. A systematic process description needs to be articulated for your (possibly unique) way in which you use the TAM to achieve your objectives. The role of the TAM in the end-to-end process of managing the customer through to the final conclusion must be fully specified. All the possible eventualities of a conversation with the customer must be thought through and legislated for in terms of:

- TAM conversation
- TAM or support team follow-up action
- Follow-up action by other units and mechanisms, and quality control to ensure that these satisfy the customer

In many circumstances, another part of your organization may be required to do something, so clear agreement must be reached with them about how this will be achieved, support resources allocated and processes agreed. If there is any uncertainty, you can be sure that your TAMs will be flooded with calls that they are unable to handle, to the dissatisfaction of both sides!

Support resources include:

- the TAM customer database
- support staff (see Chapter 6)
- support systems (see Chapter 5)
- supplies of literature, stationery, quote and contract blanks etc.
- outside resources such as demonstration facilities, field sales, order processing, order fulfilment and literature fulfilment

Of course when securing outside resources (particularly within your own organization), care must be taken to spend time getting the owners of these resources on your side. This should ensure that they will deliver to you with strong commitment.

Management processes

Managing performance

Your TAM operation must achieve a high level of motivation within a structured and controlled environment. This means that the skills required to manage the group are important, as well as the need to develop, understand and implement key performance measurements. In Chapter 6, we discussed the roles of management in relation to performance. We stated that the TAM Operations Manager (TOM) must have the process skills. The management skills in this environment (required specifically by the TAM Operations Manager) fall into the following areas:

- *Managing the TAM process* – The TAM process must be managed from start to finish, and requires a full understanding of the process itself, as well as of any marketing and management initiatives which are current within your company.
- *Managing, motivating and coaching TAM staff* – These elements are most important in the TAM environment. The TAMs will require significant attention in the early stages to ensure that they are on the right track and that their motivation is kept at a high level. You need to involve TAMs in any measurement and control methods that you use to track their performance. You will also need to measure many steps in the TAM process, so that individual TAMs can identify where they need help in improving their performance (see productivity ratios below). You must also ensure that they are informed about other customer-focused initiatives taking place in your company, as well as the need to know how they will be affected by these initiatives. Doing all this will help to maximize this motivation and to ensure an effective performance.

Key productivity ratios

In Chapter 4, we briefly covered key ratios, and likely costs and benefits. The benefits will be achieved and the costs controlled only through a structured management approach. In TAM, the old management sayings of 'You get what you inspect, not what you expect', and 'If you can't measure it, you can't manage it', apply with a vengeance. Let us examine the ratios in more detail.

Dials

Dials are the start and the essence of proactive telemanagement of customers. If TAMs are not trying to speak to customers often enough, every hour, every day, every week and every month, none of the purposes of TAM can be achieved.

Decision-maker contacts (DMCs)

Whatever role your TAMs are going to play in the sales and marketing strategies within your organization, you will need to set a target for how many decision-makers are contacted during any period and for what ratio you expect between dials and DMCs. Achieving this ratio of DMCs per day (or week) is important for two main reasons.

- It ensures that your resources are geared correctly and effectively towards the level of customer coverage that is demanded by the role you have given the TAMs.
- Measuring the number of *decision-makers* contacted ensures that your TAMs are getting through to the right level of person within the customer organization. This means that you are not just measuring activity *per se*. You are measuring (potentially) *productive* activity.

The required ratio depends on your decision-makers' habits and your TAMs' skills. If the results fall below an acceptable level (less than 1 in 5 makes the TAM job frustrating and selling rather expensive), you need to find out why. Reasons include:

- *Market factors* (competitors having tied up the market, your products not right, previous problems in relationships with your company). These are out of control of the TAM and should have been investigated earlier. The TAM should not be the victim of poor marketing planning.
- *TAM fear.* If you find a high level of 'busy' tone or 'not available' dial results for a particular TAM, listen to

their calls to verify. You may find that they are backing down at the switchboard. Fear can lead a TAM to fake dial records. To check this, compare TAM notes to ACD records.

This investigation and follow-up action (coaching, motivation, discipline) is what we mean by attention to operational detail in the TAM management role. If this is not done quickly, TAMs will not achieve the right sales and customer satisfaction results. Morale will be rapidly undermined.

Decisions and contracts sent

Measuring the ratio of:

- DMCs to customer decisions (end of the sales cycle, for good or ill)
- DMCs to number of contracts issued to customers who have agreed to buy:

gives you the information you need to drive:

- *Up* the number of calls that are active sales presentations or closes
- *Down* the number of follow-up calls per sales cycle

These measures help you see where TAMs need coaching to close sales. New or tired TAMs fear rejection, leading them to avoid asking customers to make a decision one way or the other. This makes each sale more expensive and can irritate customers (if a TAM hesitates or artificially prolongs a conversation).

Contracts returned

To ensure customers are not coerced into making wrong decisions on the phone, so that unwanted sales contracts are sent out, followed by unproductive chasing calls, measure the ratio between contracts sent and those returned signed by the customer. Aim for this ratio to be 1.0,

i.e. no unwanted contracts. More than 1.0 means call guides or TAMs need improving.

Detailed ratios

Various more detailed ratios can be used to fine tune the operation, for example:

- sales revenue per contract
- sales revenue per customer
- DMCs *vs.* literature sent
- literature sent *vs.* revenue received
- revenue per DMC
- number of orders per DMC
- product demonstrations per DMC
- revenue per product demonstration

Many others can be used. Choose ones that suit your products and your customers. These should be ratios secondary to those listed above. These must be measured for each TAM over longer and shorter time periods, to facilitate skills development and encourage personal endeavour.

Marketing definition for each TAM

Each TAM will be responsible for a specific number of customers. It is important to calculate this number carefully, as it will ultimately determine the level of market coverage you achieve, and the quality of account development. The number of customers you should allocate to each TAM depends upon the required frequency and depth of contact. The depth of contact relates to:

- the complexity of the dialogue between the TAM and the customer
- How much can be achieved in each call

For example, a TAM selling computer supplies to large companies can deal with fewer customers than a TAM dealing with life insurance and pensions for individual consumers. Note that the frequency of buying decisions exercises an important influence here.

Customer contacts

Your overall strategy should give the total number of times you would like your customers contacted each year. This will depend on several factors, including:

- the average re-order cycle for your products or services
- the rate of introduction of new or changed products/services
- the average value of each order
- the average amount of other contact you have with your customers

We believe that it is unlikely that you would wish to set up a TAM team to contact the customer base less than three times per year. It could be as often as once a week. Once you decide this, and the ideal length of each call, calculating

other productivity targets is easy, based on a dial level of 4500 dials per TAM year. That is why measuring all the above-mentioned ratios is critical for success.

Other important measures

There are two other areas that need attention: absolute performance and the quality of customer dialogue.

Absolute performance

The measurement of absolute performance (as opposed to productivity) will normally be revenue-related. An example of this would be the sales revenue generated by the customers managed by your TAMs. It is this, compared to the cost of setting up and running TAM, that will determine the viability of TAM. It is also likely to be the basis for performance comparisons and their derivative – sales competitions. However, make sure you allow for learning. Figure 8.1 shows how revenue is likely to increase in the first year of operation.

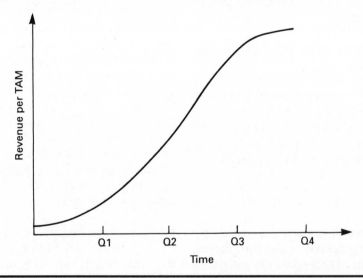

Figure 8.1 Productivity curve

You may be able to determine the link between TAM selling and sales, but if your TAM operation is working in conjunction with a sales force (however tightly or loosely), you may occasionally find that there is an argument over attribution of sales. We advise that where you think that this conflict is likely, you should agree rules in advance. These may include commission-sharing rules as well. Never allow your own channels to compete for customers – it is irritating and expensive. Remember, in the end, you want your customers to buy and be satisfied, and your sales force (TAM and field) to remain motivated. If you allow dispute over who sold what, both sales and motivation will be destroyed. We believe that if the TAM team includes some field sales staff, and is properly managed, it is relatively easy to allocate sales to individuals. Where a TAM refers a lead to the field salesperson, commission should be shared. If the field salesperson is calling only when the TAM requests, there should be no problems of 'surprising' sales made by the field salesperson alone. Finally, if the TAM is made responsible for efficient use of the field salesperson, there is little liklihood of the TAM not deploying the salesperson properly.

Quality of customer dialogue

Customer dialogue is a parameter as important as absolute performance, but is more difficult to determine because of its qualitative nature. 'Quality of the dialogue' refers to that between TAMs and their customers. To assess this quality, the TAM Operations Manager must listen regularly to telephone calls between TAMs and their customers. This can be achieved either by directly listening to live calls, or by using a tape recorder so that the calls can be listened to later. In both cases the TAMs should be informed at all times of exactly what the nature of the exercise is, and the

reasons for it. They should also be given clear criteria for quality and shown how to improve quality, as well as being encouraged to listen on their own to their tapes, (particularly after very difficult or successful calls) to understand and learn from what happened.

Feedback

To help improve the skills of the staff, and to motivate them, the standard sales management process should be adopted, as follows:

- Setting performance targets (quantitative and qualitative).
- Measuring performance against these targets.
- Feeding back the results positively to that member of staff.

Setting targets

Setting realistic targets can help ensure that the TAM unit will ultimately meet its overall objectives, and will facilitate measurement of achievement and relative progress. It will also allow the TAMs to see this progress and to be motivated accordingly. You must also assess quality. High targets on calls and sales may cause the quality of calls to drop.

The targets should be based upon experience. If you have just started using TAM, you will of course have no experience. In this case, you should obtain advice about what performance levels are reasonable and have been achieved in similar industries using TAM for similar purposes. This information should be available from reputable telemarketing consultancies and agencies.

Typically TAM targets cover the following:

- number of dials

- number of decision-maker contacts
- number of hours at the workstation
- number of sales made (or other absolute measurement)
- value of sales made
- product mix

Normal target setting rules apply Targets should:

- be realistic
- be reviewed regularly
- reflect your company's strategic direction

Targets should be increased as experience with TAM grows. Initial productivity is usually low, as both TAMs and customers are learning. As customers get used to the dialogue, and as the TAMs deploy their calling more effectively, gathering more and more information about customer needs, productivity should rise quite steeply. Make sure your targets are not so high at the start that staff become disillusioned. Increase targets from the first day onwards. Inform TAMs that you are increasing targets so they know from the beginning what they will be expected to achieve.

Incentives

As in any sales-oriented organization, the use of incentives can motivate staff and consequently drive up performance. Consider small frequent incentives for all members of the TAM team, *including the support staff*. A highly motivated sales team with a demotivated support team obviously does not work anywhere near as well as having a single, highly motivated and integrated sales/support team.

Incentives can be used to achieve both motivation and integration. They should be used wisely, so that performance relative to individual targets is recognized. In this way, both low achievers and the high-flyers can be encouraged to gain in levels of both skills and performance. But make sure that any incentive passes the test of enhancing the dialogue with customers — the subject of the next chapter.

9

The TAM dialogue with customers

A top telemarketing consultant, R.H. Oetting, was one of the leaders of the British Telecom TAM project. He believes – rightly in our view – that the telephone becomes an effective sales and marketing tool only when customers who need your products and services are contacted by trained staff, in a controlled dialogue, supported by efficiently designed systems, to a previously planned objective. This is the essence of telemanaging as we are proposing it. All aspects of the process (workflow, measurement and fulfilment) are important. But all hinge on the successful dialogue between the TAM and the customer. This is the point where information is passed between you and your customers – the point where products and services are bought and sold.

We now look at how TAMs perform their account management role, and cover in detail issues relating to productivity. A better understanding of TAMs and their role within the operation will result in a better understanding of the importance of effective support and management of the total TAM process.

The TAM's role

TAMs are primarily salespeople. They operate tried and tested sales procedures, using skills that they either already have or have learned on their various training courses. As salespeople, they must sell a certain amount of services or products. As account managers they must establish a relationship with their customers and understand their needs, so as to increase your company's business with them.

Because of the unique nature of communicating over the telephone, TAMs need special communications skills – skills of listening, being able to explain complex concepts clearly and succinctly, and being able to convey a warm and friendly manner and thus establish a relationship with the customer. To help in this process we suggest the use of call guides, to guide the TAM through the call. These should follow the traditional steps of the sale to ensure that the call is a success.

The steps are as follows:

1 Preparation
2 Introduction
3 Opening the sale
4 Needs analysis
5 Presentation of solutions
6 Explanation of the benefits
7 Trial close
8 Overcoming objections/answering questions

9 Close
10 Confirming commitment
11 Preparing the way for the next call

Call guides

At the heart of the TAM process is the call guide, which should be prepared by someone who understands:

- the role of the TAM on the phone
- the target market
- the products being sold

The guides should be tested before they are released.

Call guides can be presented to the TAMs on paper, or they can be programmed into a computerized system. Most computerized telemarketing systems allow programming of customized call guides.

The call guide allows TAMs to navigate their way through the call, giving prompts and support at every stage, including prompting on product benefits and prices, as well as providing possible answers to tricky objections.

The benefits of using call guides (from a management perspective) include:

- providing the TAM with a structured dialogue, thus ensuring that all possible points are covered
- easing the training process, as TAMs use call guides to help them sell new products
- giving TAMs confidence and professionalism quickly, so increasing the productivity of the TAM process
- standardization and adherence to specific marketing approaches without loss of either techniques or skills

For the TAM, the call guide provides the following:

- A chance to listen attentively to the customer without worrying about what to say next.
- Clear signs to the TAM as to their exact position within a call, regardless of the number of seemingly similar calls made before that particular one. This applies even when a customer takes a different tack during a call. A TAM can be 'side-tracked' by the customer (to mutual benefit) without losing the thread. This ensures the objective of the call is met.
- The opportunity to close more business as a result of a more thorough sales approach.
- The availability of detailed product information allowing them to answer many of the customer's questions there and then.
- The ability to enter answers to relevant questions speedily via the same screen as the call guide and store those answers automatically on the database for future use.

The TAM should always be in control of the situation. Call guides help considerably in this respect. For this reason, it is usually the good TAMs who use the call guides most effectively.

A different set of guides should be created for each situation that TAMs may find themselves in (see Figure 9.1). This includes having specific product or service benefits included in each set. Call guide sets should be modular. In this way, duplication is minimized and flexibility maximized. A wide product portfolio can be managed more easily too. The modular approach requires logical links and signposts between modules to help TAMs chart the most productive path between them during a conversation. If you computerize your call guides, you can hide the logical links and let the sequence of events determine the selection of the next path for the conversation automatically. The most advanced systems here incorporate

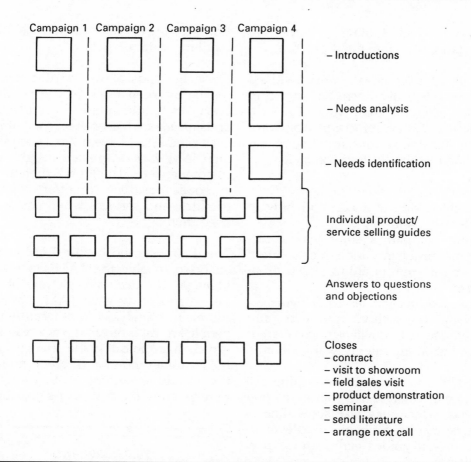

Campaign 1   Campaign 2   Campaign 3   Campaign 4

– Introductions

– Needs analysis

– Needs identification

Individual product/
service selling guides

Answers to questions
and objections

Closes
– contract
– visit to showroom
– field sales visit
– product demonstration
– seminar
– send literature
– arrange next call

Figure 9.1 TAM call guide set

expertise, so the system can analyse the results of past conversations and learn from them which modules and links work best, i.e. what is the best path through a conversation for customers of particular kinds who give particular responses.

Regardless of the sophistication or medium for presenting the call guide (computer or paper), each call guide set should allow the TAM to:

- identify and reach the decision maker
- accept detours the customer wants
- determine the decision maker's needs and identify opportunities
- offer solutions

- handle questions and objections effectively
- keep the door open at the end of the call

The TAM's confidence in selecting and using call guides will quickly increase with experience. In the TAMs' first training sessions, considerable practice in using call guides should be given. To someone new to telemarketing, using a call guide can seem artificial – a feeling that can easily be transmitted to the customer. The essence of the account management relationship is that it should feel natural. If the customer, who may be quite a senior business person, feels he is the subject of a scripted 'telesales' call, the relationship will take off on a bad footing. Hence the importance of training and practice.

Do not underestimate the work involved in developing call guides. You may find it more difficult than you expect to extract clarity and precision from product managers, sector marketing managers and the like, on topics such as:

- product portfolio planning
- likely customer needs and how to identify them
- your company's solutions to customer problems, and which solution is most appropriate to which problem
- key product and service benefits
- likely competitive products and companies that will be encountered, and good arguments against them

In fact, the very activity of writing call guides may catalyse a deeper marketing analysis, which may take some time to produce results. So begin the development of call guides early, and expect problems.

Customer information

Basic customer information should be held for every customer the TAM is calling. This information is enhanced by the TAM during the conversation with the customer. Call guides should be structured so that the answers to questions posed by the TAM can be readily entered onto the customer database, if possible as they are being given by the customer. In this way the database is automatically updated upon completion of the call.

If direct database entry is not possible, a system must be developed for the database to be updated at another stage, probably by the support staff. If so, paper records must be completed by

TAMs during the call and then passed on for filing or data input.

These methods allow the database to constantly keep track of the result of every call attempted, whether the decision-maker has been reached or not. Each time a TAM speaks to a customer, the TAM has a greater insight into customer needs. The TAM is therefore in a good position to offer relevant products and services when customers need them.

The data collected by the TAM can be analysed to give the TAM Operations Manager an accurate picture of the calling profile for each TAM. The data can also be analysed to determine why people are *not* interested. As a result we can change the call guide strategy, give the customer more or different information or add something to the call guide to respond to the customer's objection.

Measurements

You must measure and monitor both the quantitative and qualitative aspects of the TAM operation. As indicated in Chapter 8, quantitative measurements include:

- number and result of all calls made
- number of hours spent on the phone
- resultant revenue achieved

Qualitative measurements are associated with the actual call itself. Here the TOM monitors live calls and the TAM tapes calls for subsequent review. They also relate to information passed to the customer via other fulfilment media (e.g. literature, letters, quotes and contracts).

Measurements are needed to:

- identify problem areas that need improvement

- project achievable results
- determine which markets/lists/ strategies have been successful
- let the whole team know where they have been and where they are going

A critical element of TAM productivity measurement is the 'TAM phone-hour', the number of hours that TAMs spend sitting at their workstations managing customer accounts over the telephone in any one day. The TAM phone-hour is not just how long the TAM spends actually talking on the phone. It includes time spent preparing for a call, and time spent immediately after the call on matters related specifically to that call. It does not include lunchtime, teatime, any breaks, meetings, training, etc.

In Table 9.1 is shown the breakdown of a typical TAM's average time spent using the telephone within an average TAM phone-hour. It is for a TAM operation in which the average TAM completes 5 phone-hours per day, achieves 75 dials (attempts) from which 25 decision-makers are reached. The averages will vary according to a number of factors, not least being

the individual TAMs themselves.

It can be seen that a typical TAM spends less than half the phone-hour using the phone, and only about one-third of the phone-hour talking to customers.

Remember, other factors affecting the averages include:

- complexity of product/service being sold
- value of product/service being sold
- stage of evolution of the TAM process in the organization
- level of awareness the customer has of the organization and/or the product or service

Each combination results in different call times (the call guides are different and calls will last different times). These need to be worked into the objectives for each TAM at each stage in the TAM programme. The productivity of each TAM is then regularly tracked throughout each campaign and compared with their objectives, for both control and bonus purposes.

Table 9.1 TAM phone time

Call set-up time	= 10 seconds per call	= (10 × 15) =	150 seconds
Average ring time	= 15 seconds per call	= (15 × 15) =	225 seconds
Unanswered calls (2 per hour at 15 seconds each)		= (2 × 15) =	30 seconds
Total non-connected time		=	405 seconds
		=	6 mins 45 seconds
Answered calls	8 DM (decision maker) not available	(30 seconds extra) =	240 seconds
4/5 DM (decision maker) contacts		(3 × 90 seconds) =	270 seconds
		(2 × 5 minutes) =	600 seconds
Total time connected per phone-hour		=	1110 seconds
		=	18 mins 30 seconds

So total connect plus non-connect time per phone-hour
6 minutes 45 seconds + 18 minutes 30 seconds = 25 minutes 5 seconds

87

out each campaign and compared with their objectives, for both control and bonus purposes.

The TAM process

The TAM process involves planning, implementing and monitoring full account management of the TAM customer base. All members of the TAM operation – the TAM Operations Manager, the TAMs themselves and the TAM Support Team - have a vital role to play in the effective operation of the TAM process.

At first, your main source of customer information, and hence initial prompts to call customers, comes from the main customer database. There are other reasons, however, for TAMs to call customers. These include the following:

Scheduled follow-up calls

Follow-up calls will be scheduled by the TAM as part of the sales cycle with customers that have previously been contacted by the TAM or have contacted the TAM previously themselves. Most computerized systems will automatically set a call-back depending on the algorithm set for the type of close. TAMs may override this and set their own callback date if they feel that this is appropriate. On the other hand, a paper-based system will need to have this 'follow-up call' diary process as a fundamental part of it.

Some follow-up calls may well be the result of some activity outside the TAM unit. In this case the call is made when the activity has been completed, and not strictly scheduled by the TAM. Examples of this type of external activity

include the receipt of a signed contract, or notification that a sales visit has been completed.

For new TAM operations, follow-up calls and initial list-generated calls should form the bulk of the TAM's calling initially.

After-sales calls

After-sales calls are scheduled by the TAM to take place at a predetermined time after a proposed installation or other order fulfilment (e.g. arrival of the product, start of a service) is scheduled to take place. The purpose of these calls is to get the TAM to:

- confirm that the order was successfully fulfilled
- check that the customer is happy
- consolidate the customer's trust in the TAM's judgement
- sell further products or services, if appropriate

Leads from other sales units or from marketing campaigns

As the TAM operation evolves, there will be an increase in the number of enquiries coming into the TAM operation from other sales units which believe that the TAM operation is better qualified to deal with them. This lead passing should be encouraged as soon as the TAM operation is capable of handling all types of customer call. If necessary, commission sharing arrangments should be established.

Promotional direct mail, seminar or advertising campaigns may generate leads from TAM customers. These must be fitted into the calling schedule.

In/outbound calls – fully account managed

After an initial period, the concept and practice of telemanagement will be well established with the customer base. At this stage the TAMs will be planning their own calling cycles according to the needs of their customers. Pure list-generated calling will cease (other than the normal product launch or similar marketing campaigns) and true account management will take over. TAMs will be making and receiving calls from fully account managed customers.

From an early stage, however, some TAM customers will be calling in. We suggest that the support staff are set up and trained to receive all inbound calls. This will allow them to filter these calls. Various possibilities exist here:

- the call can be handled by the support person directly
- the call can be handled by someone else outside the TAM unit
- the call requires the TAM to call the customer

In each case, the support person should ensure that the customer record is updated accordingly. In this way, the TAM will always be making pre-prepared outbound calls, thus maximizing efficiency and effectiveness.

In the longer term, you may want to have a single point of contact for all calls from customers, passing those requiring call-backs from the TAMs directly to the TAM operation. In this way the TAMs will be treated as a dedicated sales channel. This single reception point for all sales, service and billing enquiries could become part of an integrated sales channel strategy across your company.

Outcomes of a TAM call

There are three broad categories of outcome when a TAM calls a customer. They are:

- no contact is made
- contact is made with a non-decision-maker
- contact is made with a decision-maker

The following table on p.90 (Table 9.2) is a list of all possible call results, the associated codes and a brief description of each. (See also call outcomes introduced in Chapter 3). These codes are suggestions, and any existing, or similar ones may well be more appropriate in your organization.

Whatever coding system you use, all the code definitions must have significance for measurement, i.e. a measurement on any one code which is significantly higher or lower than target should imply some action. For example, too many mis-dials may indicate carelessness or problems with the equipment. No mis-dials should indicate cause for congratulation of the individual or team concerned. The use of ratios has already been discussed in Chapter 8.

Obviously, codes are entered as a matter of trust. However, the ability of the manager to listen to any call and (in a fully computerized system) to see the result being entered, should militate against falsification of results. Also, if every measure is significant, there is little incentive to falsify. Entering as a mis-dial a failed call which took a long time leaves time to be accounted for elsewhere. Intelligent TAMs will realize that falsification of code entry could quickly produce a tangle from which it would be very difficult to extract themselves.

OUTCOME	CALL CODE	DESCRIPTION
DMC (decision-maker contacts)		
Sales decision	C	Sales contract will be sent to the customer
Confirmed sale	CS	Customer has mailed or will return contract
Not interested now	NIN	No sales interest in products discussed but still interested in account management
Not interested at all	NO	Not interested in any products, nor in account management. Do not promote
Send literature	SL	Send literature
Call-back for decision	CBFD	Any call back *to a decision-maker* not covered by SL, CS, S, V, D, NIN, NO, SQ
Visit requested	V	Sales visit scheduled
Demonstration	D	Product demonstration arranged
Service call	SC	1 A call to, or from, the customer that has no sales intent (e.g. to advise of an installation date) 2 A scheduled call back to a customer after installation or other fulfilment of order
Send quotation	SQ	Quotation will be sent to the customer
Non-DMC		
Time available	TA	No decision-maker contact but a precise time for a call-back has been established
Call programmed	CP	No precise time for call has been established but a generic time slot (a.m. or p.m.) has been established
Not qualified	NQ	Decision-making responsibility exists outside the TAM operation's territory
Refusal	R	Switchboard or other refuses to connect with decision-maker
Referral	RE	1 TAM either referred to another office within the operation's territory for purchasing authority or a colleague within the same organization 2 A customer refers a TAM to an associate in another organization
No Contact		
Did not answer	DA	No response to ringing tone
List error	L	Duplicate record, someone else's customer
No connection	N	No connection achieved, no ringing tone
Mis-dial	M	Wrong number dialled (noted either during or after dialling)
Engaged	E	Number engaged

Management reports should group these calls in the above way (DMC, non-DMC, no contact), as this gives a very quick, clear picture of the effectiveness of the targeting and of the management of the sales cycle. You may use other groupings to produce other measures of effectiveness, for example:

Total decisions	NIN + NO + C
Non-sales, service, follow-up	CS + SC
Incompletes	SL + SQ + V + D + CBFD
Errors	M + L + NQ
Total DMCs	CS + SC + NIN + NO + C + SL + SQ + V + D + CBFD

Table 9.2 Possible call results

Next action

In most cases, the next action to be taken will be obvious from the call result code. Where the call results in the need for a subsequent call-back, either the computerized system will automatically schedule the call-back dependent on the result code (TAMs should be able to override the automatic timing of call-backs if required), or the paper-based system should enable the support staff to bring forward the customer file when the call-back is due.

The connection between the call result code and the next action will also be determined by the contact strategy. For example, if the result was 'Send literature', the contact strategy may indicate a call-back after two weeks (allowing time for sending, delivery and reading).

Updating the database

Once a call cycle has been completed, when the customer has decided either that they will definitely buy – or will definitely *not* buy – some product or service from your organization, then this information should be fed back into the customer database. This, of course, assumes you have such a database – the subject of the next chapter.

10

Using computers

In previous chapters we have discussed use of word processors and personal computers to help the support team, the use of ACDs to manage, record and log the calls made both into and out of the TAM operation, and have considered the TAM process and the necessary use of a database as a core part of that process. We have also discussed the support necessary to maintain the TAM process, and mentioned the advantages of computerized call guides. We now consider computerization of that part of the TAM process which physically involves the TAMs themselves. This part of the process can be (and often is) computerized by readily-available, standard packages. In practice, however, even these standard packages need to be tailored to some extent.

Standard packages are sold under the generic title of 'telemarketing systems' and run on anything from a personal computer to a mainframe. Some only perform telemarketing functions, while others offer a whole range of extra functions such as territory planning and sales accounting. Almost all have some form of database manager facility as a common factor linking all the offered functions.

The price of systems varies enormously, depending on which you choose, and how many users will be operational at any one time. The smallest will cost a few hundred pounds for software to run on an existing personal computer. The largest (1990 prices) will cost up to £10,000 ($15,000) per workstation, including the cost of all the hardware and software.

Where possible, involve the services of any local expert (preferably independent, probably from your own organization) who can help you determine:

- what it is best to computerize and what not to
- which system to choose once you have decided what you want

The TAM process must be clearly designed, specified and tested before you attempt to computerize any part of it. Several companies have designed, specified and implemented the process, running for anything up to a year without computerizing. They do this in order to pilot the approach and get it right before computerizing. In fact, it may even be an option not to computerize at all, and would certainly depend on the number of TAMs you were employing, the number of customers each TAM looked after, the frequency of calling each customer and the complexity of your product portfolio.

A computerized telemarketing system

can be used to computerize the complete process. To do this, you would need to computerize every single aspect – call guides, calling prompts, database, reporting, fulfilment and accounting. All members of the TAM team should have access to it. This approach would be most suitable for a smaller organization, or a larger organization where the TAM operation is the prime (if not only) channel of communication and sales. This is characteristic of mail-order companies selling off a catalogue.

A telemarketing system could also be used as a stand-alone TAM system, linking the database with the main company database. In this case, sales/order processing would take place elsewhere, on another computer. This option would be more likely in a larger organization where the TAM unit was not the only sales channel. Integration with sales processing systems (order entry, inventory control) and service systems should always be your eventual target, allowing you to guarantee delivery and installation dates, and give up-to-date information on product availability. However, reliable on-line integration is not easy to achieve. If your company has a history of problems with system integration, approach this topic carefully. Consider interim solutions, such as (daily) batch updates, until you are certain you can make the integration work.

Computerized telemarketing coverage

The four main areas covered by most computerized telemarketing systems are:

- information management
- call management
- fulfilment
- performance analysis

Information management

Current information about each customer, such as name, address, telephone number, is held on the system's database along with details of all previous contacts (for example, name of TAM, which literature was sent, quotations sent, purchases made) together with information gathered during the needs analysis carried out by the TAMs. TAMs can individually access records from their own list of designated customers by name or telephone number. Lists can also be put together using a variety of marketing criteria such as time of last contact, location or interest shown in a particular product.

Call management

The telemarketing system manages calls by the use of lists, such as an initial campaign list. Once the first call to each customer is made the system's diary facility takes over, allowing TAMs to set their own call-back time, as well as providing an automatic scheduling facility for calls which are initially engaged or where there is no answer.

At the start of each day, the telemarketing system presents the TAMs with a list of scheduled calls to be made that day. It also allows the TAM to have access to the current campaign list. On most systems, calls are managed via interactive call guides. These start with a needs analysis to ensure that the required information is gathered from each customer in a structured and consistent manner. The facility to use call guides, scripts or prompts is offered on most telemarketing systems. However, you will need to design and write your own guides and either have them programmed into the system, or key them in yourself.

TAMs sit at the screen of the telemarketing system and are prompted as to what to say to the customer. The system can be programmed with (if necessary) complex logic so that the TAM is steered to the relevant part of the guide depending on what the customer has said in reply. This process is called *decision-tree prompting*. TAMs key in these replies from the customer directly onto the screen, and a record is therefore kept for later use, either during that call, or in subsequent calls.

TAMs also have access to other call guides, including those which are product-specific or for objection handling. They should be able to access any information on the system (customer information on the database, information from previous calls, information from this call). The level of flexibility for call-guide construction, length, branching and cross-referencing varies between systems. The more expensive systems offer more choice. Take the costs and benefits of greater flexibility into account in your purchasing decision.

Note that your TAM database may need to be transferred to your main database, to be used by other sales or communication channels. You need to consider this possibility at the outset. Your decision will influence the size of the database the TAM system needs, its data structure, and interface requirements.

Fulfilment

Personalized letters can be generated by some systems, either for local fulfilment or via a mailing house. Data for fulfilment can often be transmitted either over an electronic link or via a magnetic tape, directly to the fulfilment house so that they can send personalized letters and specific literature pieces directly to the customer.

Performance analysis

Telemarketing systems usually offer a large variety of reports which measure most aspects of TAM performance and productivity. This ensures that TOMs have the correct information at the right time to enable leading, motivating, training, coaching, organizing and planning the TAM team. We recommend that all this reporting be computerized and produced automatically, saving on clerical resource, and meaning that TAMs do not have to worry about it.

Choosing a system

The systems which are currently available are software packages, supplied by a variety of software developers and distributors both in the UK and the USA. Most are advertised as telemarketing systems, and all require specific hardware to allow them to run. The larger software systems usually require dedicated hardware, although a number of smaller systems can run on personal computers along with other software packages.

Go through the following five steps when choosing your telemanaging system.

1. Define your requirements

This is a key step, whether you are considering computerizing your TAM process or not. Define the TAM process for your organization from start to finish. Include what you want from the system for the whole process, including management reporting facilities. Use the description of a typical system to guide you, and include your thoughts and limits on price. Think about the longer term, when considering the price as you may wish to choose a system now that will accommodate your expansion in the future. Consider whether each facility is a necessity or just nice to have, and whether it is worth paying for.

Think also about what type of supplier you are looking for. The system specification is important, but so are items such as training, installation support, on-going support and general attitude of the supplier. Also their past history should reveal their future capability to supply the sort of complete system that you will want.

2. Get an expert to help

Experts will help, especially if you have no previous experience of choosing computer systems. Often someone with a computer background in your own company can help, and is especially important if either you have to choose a large system, (and therefore may have to spend a large amount of money) or if your TAM system has to interface with other systems within your organization. Another person could be a telemarketing consultant who has had previous experience in choosing such systems.

3. Create a shortlist

Once you decide what you want, create a shortlist of possible suppliers. This can be done by approaching others who have already chosen telemarketing systems, or by checking in telemarketing, direct marketing and database marketing magazines. These will be the suppliers that you invite to tender against the specification that you have drawn up (see Step 1).

4. Review the shortlist

Consider the following when you are reviewing:

- ask for a demonstration of the system, preferably together with your expert
- ask for local reference sites that you can visit; try and see their operations; choose sites similar to your planned operation
- check for any hidden costs such as installation costs, training costs, costs of extra hardware
- ask suppliers to answer all your predetermined requirements; be willing to change these as you see other systems, but be objective at all times

5. Choose your system and your supplier

At the end of the day, it is *your* decision. Choose suppliers that you feel most comfortable with. Be straight with them and expect them to be straight with you. Once you have chosen, do not change your mind, or start compromising. This can lead to very long delays, and you might still not end up with what you want.

What the system must outperform – the paper-based system

If you want to pilot telemanagement in the safest way, involving the least investment and lowest chance of errors caused by systems, you need to design a fairly comprehensive paper-based process. If you go straight to a computerized system, whether off-the-peg or customized, that system will need to emulate the output of the paper-based system, even if the way it works is very different.

Running a paper-based system is support-intensive. Much of the work of support staff is in ensuring that proper filing takes place. This includes taking out files for the TAM's attention, recording results, and replacing files. Computerization reduces the need for much of this filing work, allowing support staff to concentrate on matters such as sales-order processing and mailing. This too should be computerized as much as possible, but some support staff will always be needed.

Contact and dialling records

There are two central records in the paper-based process. One is customer-orientated, and called the *contact record*. One contact record is associated with each calling cycle for each customer. The relationship with each customer is therefore conducted through a series of contact records. The other is internal operations-oriented, and relates to each TAM's dialling activity. It is called the *dialling record*.

The contact filing system

Because each TAM should be dealing with a large number of customers, the filing system is the key to proper customer management. In fact, the filing system has two 'cabinets':

- an *open* cabinet, where contact records and associated paperwork are filed during the calling cycle or while the calling cycle is open
- a *closed* cabinet, where all customer information is filed between calling cycles or when the cycle is closed

The open filing system

This allows contact records and related customer information to be held in 'next action' categories, in date order. It ensures that:

- any record can be found easily
- TAMs are prompted to make call backs at the right time
- any situation requiring action by TAM support staff or others in your company is readily picked up and passed to the TAM as soon as that action has taken place

The filing system has a set of open files for each TAM, using a shelf-based system (see Figure 10.1) arranged as pigeon holes. Each must be large enough to take at least a one-inch high pile of A4 paper.

The boxes are defined as follows:

1 *Contract issued:* Contract has been sent to the customer and a call-back is programmed for 7 days after the contract is issued, or when the contract is returned (whichever earlier).
2 *Quote issued:* Quote has been sent to the customer and a call-back programmed for 7 days after its issue, or when the quote is accepted (whichever earlier).
3 *Demonstration:* A product demonstration has been scheduled and a call-back programmed for the day after this scheduled date.
4 *Call-back programmed:* Any call-back that does not fit any of the other categories is filed here.
5 *Literature sent:* Literature has been sent and a call-back scheduled for 7 days after.
6 *Service call:* A sale has been made and a call-back scheduled for 10 days after the planned delivery/installation date.
7 *Sales visit:* A sales visit has been arranged and the TAM will call the

Records held in date order of next TAM call back	Contract issued	Quote issued	Demon-stration	Call back programmed
	Literature sent	Service call	Sales visit	Engaged/ No answer

Records to be closed	Sale closed	Not interested	List error	No contact
Records await-ing next action	Support ACTION required	Awaiting order processing	Awaiting technical approval	Awaiting lease clearance

Figure 10.1 Open case filing system

customer as soon as possible after the visit. Support staff will chase any sales leads given to the sales force if no visit has been arranged.

8   *Engaged/no answer:* A call-back is scheduled for later that day or the next day. If there is still no response, then calls should be made alternating between morning and afternoon until a response is achieved.

9   *Sale closed:* The sale has been closed, the order processed and the product or service has been delivered or commenced. The case is now awaiting input to the closed filing system.

10   *Not interested/list error/no contact:* Case awaiting input into closed filing system for any of these three reasons.

11   *Support action required:* Next step involves some action by support staff, e.g. sending literature/ contract/quote, booking a product demonstration, order processing, internal progress chasing. Once the task has been completed, the papers are placed in the relevant awaiting action slot.

12   *Awaiting order processing/technical approval/lease clearance:* The next stage after Step 11.

A computerized system must also use these categories. If an icon-based interface is used, it can emulate the physical interface, giving TAMs a complete overview of their workload in one screen, particularly if the number of cases in each box is shown.

Figure 10.2 shows the possible relationship between call result codes, time lags and the open filing system.

Closed filing and the database

Once a calling or sales cycle is closed, customer records must be filed in a closed file, until the customer makes a call or the next outbound call is scheduled (for the next sales cycle). If TAM-derived information is being logged on your main customer database, you must ensure that customer status is also recorded. Figure 10.3 shows how

TAM result code	Time lag for next action	'Open' file
C	Call back after 7 days	Contract issued
CS	Call back after 3 days	Contract issued
NIN	Schedule for next calling cycle	Not interested
NO	Do not call again	Not interested
SL	Call back after 7 days	Literature sent
CBFD	Call back as agreed	Call back
V	Call back after visit	Sales visit
D	Call back after demonstration	Demonstration
SC	Call back 10 days after product/ service commences	Service call
SQ	Call back after 7 days	Quote issued
TA/CP	Call back as agreed	Call back
NQ	No further call	List error
R	No further call	No contact
RE	Call back by new TAM	New TAM file
DA/E	Call back next day, then regularly (a.m./p.m.) up to 3 months	No contact
L	No further call	List error

Figure 10.2 Open files, codes and time lags

customer status might be coded on the database, together with the open file status.

Recording the results of calls

Every time a TAM makes a call, the results are recorded in at least two places – the contact record and on the dialling record – using the call result code. Hence the value of computerization, which reduces this number to one!

The support staff take the completed contact and dialling records at the end of each day and file them according to the result code in the open filing cabinet. Support staff note the next action required and schedule it in the workload for the TAM at the right time. This ensures that the contact record is extracted from the cabinet on the right day.

Tam call result code	Description	'Open' file	Database code
C	Sales contract returned and order has been processed	Sale closed	S
NIN	Not interested now	Not interested	Y
NO	Not interested at all	Not interested	N
L	List error	List error	L
NQ	Not qualified	List error	L
DA/E	No answer, engaged	No contact	U

Figure 10.3 Database statuses

Forms

One of the major disadvantages of the paper-based approach is the number of forms required to ensure clear communication. However, the use and modification of these forms during a pilot provides valuable guidance on what information is needed to run the operation. This provides important data for the specifications for computerization so you should only move straight to computerization if you are certain that you know what information needs to be passed to whom. Some companies have computerized successfully straight away, so whether you decide to do it depends mostly on your need to get things right for customers, and the degree of experience your staff have with computerized systems and with telemanaging customers.

The forms you may require include:

- *Contact record forms* – these may be printed off your main company customer database, with customer details already on them, or you may create them locally from any list.
- *Dialling record forms* – showing what calls were made, with what results.

The above two forms should be classified by the type of campaign or cycle involved. As the totals can be checked against ACD records, the TAM must enter every call under its correct timing and result:

- Customer order form – specifying the customer and product details.
- Lead notification to other sales staff (i.e. outside the TAM operation).
- Lead notification to the TAM operation from other sales units.
- Quotation/contract request – for support staff to provide a formal quote or to make out a contract of sale.
- Support staff action request – other than the above. These might include

finding a contact record, getting case papers from another department, inserting information in the case papers, booking a demonstration or sales visit, and checking progress with delivery or installation.
- General action request – to staff other than support staff, usually outside the TAM operation, e.g. a service department.
- Weekly/monthly productivity report form, covering the productivity of each TAM and allowing easy comparison between TAMs, customer groups, test groups.
- Document order form.
- Request for fulfilment literature to be sent.

Checklists are also required to ensure that every step of certain actions has taken place. These include:

- A sale checklist for TAMs.
- A monitoring checklist for TAM operations managers – this is used to give feedback to TAMs on the quality of their calls. Formal reviews should be held by the operations manager with each of the TAMs separately. Tape recordings of calls should be played back at these reviews. Scoring can be undertaken with the TAM or by the manager. These scores should be reviewed against past and peer performance.

Log books

You also need logs of sales documentation. One, the sales log book, should contain copies of all signed contracts for each TAM. You need a separate log book for outstanding contracts, which are waiting for customers to sign and return them. As they are returned signed, the contracts should be moved to the sales log book. You also need a leads log book, based on leads forms. Log books are also needed for any face-to-face contacts (e.g.

visits to showrooms, sales force visits). In the front of all log books, a status sheet should be kept, with one line for each form, summarizing its details. Log books help you follow up specific sales and leads that are not being progressed quickly and to find the details of any sale quickly.

The support routine

The paper-based system will fail if support staff do not observe strict discipline when it comes to their daily routine. Once again, if you opt for the computerized approach, your system must create the same discipline for the TAMs, with limited staff support. The routine should be something like that in Figures 10.4 and 10.5.

1 *Check open file*
Open files contain contact records due for a call-back by the TAM. Support staff take out all the contact records that have call-backs scheduled for the current date (see Figure 10.2). They should be prioritized according to state of advance of the sales cycle (or other business priority which you give). For example, customers with sales contracts ready to be signed might be top priority. These might be followed by customers who have had quotes issued to them, and so on. Added to these should be customers who were not available at the last call and those for whom there is a timed call-back scheduled.

2 *Add new contact records*
As sales cycles are finished, new ones are started. Additional contact should be initiated, to start new sales cycles with telemanaged customers. The number of new contact records to be extracted to add to the TAMs workload for the day depends on the existing call-back workload. Statistics will show how many minutes of call-back work is likely to be generated by the existing call-back load.

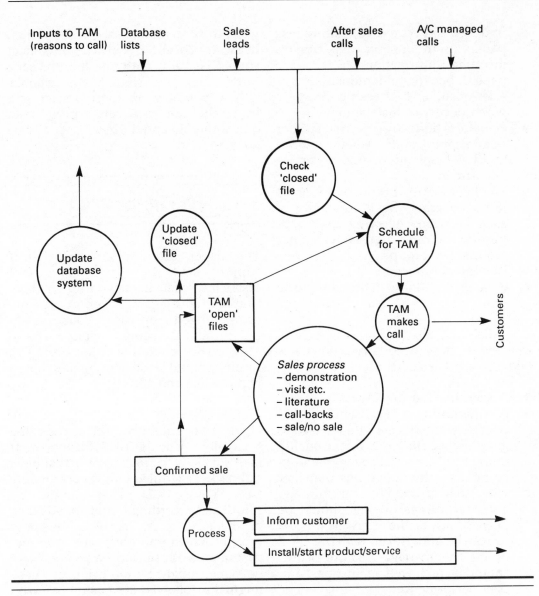

Figure 10.4 The TAM support system

These new contact records should all be closed. That is to say, none of them should have open files for other products, unless you have a campaign to run which does not conflict with the existing contact.

3 *Distribute contact records to TAMs*
Distribution means arranging them properly in a predetermined sequence at the TAMs workstation. The new contract records will have the lowest priority.

4 *Check TAM operation mail*
Check mail from customers (e.g. signed contracts) and from internal sources of leads or information.

5 *Match mail with contact records and update*
Matching ensures that data arriving in the mail that relates to contact records is duly recorded on the contact record.

6 *Distribute relevant contact records to TAMs*
Distribution means allocating contact

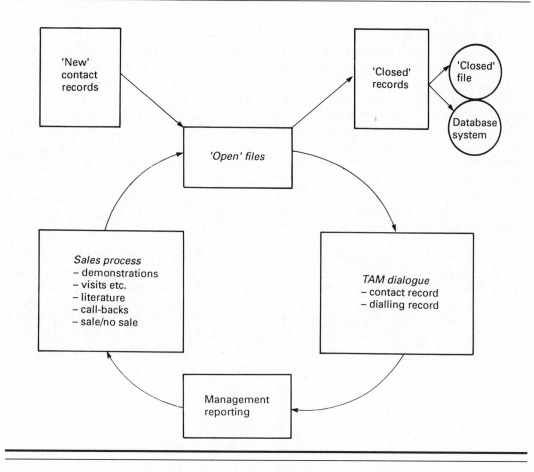

Figure 10.5 TAM 'Open' loop

records changed by the incoming mail to the TAMs work schedule.

7 *Check and carry out actions required by TAMs*

The forms stating action required by TAMs should be examined, and the actions scheduled and carried out.

8 *Total dialling records*

Totalling here requires the calls and result codes on each TAM's dialling record from the previous day to be totalled and checked.

9 *Total ACD records*

Totalling here requires checking and totalling the ACD records for each TAM for the previous day, noting the total number of phone hours for each TAM.

10 *Check revenues*

The revenue totals for each TAM which were calculated the previous day should be checked (see Step 12).

11 *Input totals to reporting system*

We are assuming that even if the operation is manual, there will be a microcomputer-based reporting system at work. This enables totals for each TAM to be cumulated, compared and reported.

12 *Process signed contracts*

All sales contracts counter-signed by the TAMs the previous day should be checked and processed according to your sales order processing rules.

13 *Process information for commissions*

Information on sales made will be needed to calculate commission due to each TAM, to any field sales staff working for the TAM operation, and for the operation as a whole. This should be processed through your usual system.

14 *File all closed cases*

Any sales cycles which have ended with no sale being made should be recorded and the paperwork filed in the closed file under the customer name. The contact records should be annotated to this effect, and all other relevant papers filed. Sales cycles which have ended with a sale should be scheduled for a call-back after delivery of the product to the customer, and after that will be filed in the closed file. The contact records are now closed until re-opened by a new sales cycle.

15 *Collect and file contact records and the rest of the day's papers*

At the close of business, all contact and dialling records and forms should be collected from TAMs. Contact records should be filed by call-back date and a record kept of contact records filed in this way.

16 *Close the office*

Sensitive customer data have been processed on paper during the day, and should all be properly filed away, under lock and key.

Apart from the last step (and perhaps even that in a few years' time!), your system must be able to do all the above tasks if your TAM operation is to be fully automated. If any elements still need to be done manually, the costs of doing this and ways to do it efficiently must be examined closely.

All the above focuses on the technical aspects of a TAM's work. But we should not forget that, apart from confirmed orders coming in from customers, there is an enduring, more personal record of the dialogue – the letter the TAM sends to the customer. These are covered in the next chapter.

11

Corresponding with customers

Running a TAM operation means dealing with much detail. If the TAM is to be productive, then the detail should be automated as far as possible. Because nearly every call will result in a letter being sent out, standard letters should be prepared to meet most eventualities: here we give examples of these letters and comment on why we believe they will be needed.

The standard letters are similar to those that have been found useful in telemanaging customers. Material in italics and within square brackets should be modified as appropriate. You will obviously need to analyse them. If your operation is a large one, these letters should be held by the fulfilment house, which will also hold digitized TAM signatures. If yours is a smaller operation, your support staff may carry out this role using word-processing equipment.

For the reader unaccustomed to direct marketing procedure, two terms are worth explaining:

- Salutation. The form of the customer's name, eg. Mr Smith, Jones. Ideally, the TAM and customer will move to first name terms eventually, at the customer's invitation.
- Toll-free. The telephone number for customers to call without charge (0800 in the UK, 800 in the US). This is an excellent way to increase customer satisfaction at low cost.

Examples

Examples of standard letters follow.

Product sale letter

> Your company name
> Company Address
> Toll free telephone number
> Date

Dear [*Salutation*],

Following our telephone conversation on [*date*], I should like to thank you for taking the time to discuss your order with me. I enclose our [*order confirmation or sales contract*]. Please sign and return it as soon as possible.

As your account manager, my objective is to help you make the very best use of [*your company*]'s products and services. I shall therefore be calling you in a few days to confirm that you have received the [*order confirmation or sales contract*] and to answer any questions you may have.

As you know, I am available whenever you want to place orders, discuss requirements, arrange product demonstrations or visits by you to us or vice versa. Do not hesitate to call me free of charge on [*toll-free number*].

For any other enquiries you may have, such as service calls and invoicing, call the following numbers:

Service calls   [*service number*]
Invoicing   [*customer administration number*]
Other queries   [*general number*]

Thank you once again for your order. I look forward to being able to help you again in the near future.

Yours sincerely,

[*TAM name*]
Account manager

Note

Because telemanaged customers will only receive a fully customized letter when you write to them, when they request literature or when they order from you, it makes sense to remind them of their contact details. They are most likely to need these details when they are about to or have just ordered from you, so it is only common courtesy to remind them of the details then. It also makes sense to remind them what your role is. This has an additional benefit – if customers move job, and someone new takes over your customers' relationship with your company, there is no need to search back in their files to find out how your company deals with them. The customer only has to look at the last letter.

If your company is large, you may have to give several other telephone numbers. Although ideally there should be one or at the most two contact numbers, we recognize that companies with very complex products and extensive relationships with their customers will find it difficult to achieve this. For this reason, the numbers should be clearly stated and published in all correspondence.

After-sales letter

Your company name
Company address
Toll-free telephone number
Date

Dear [*Salutation*],

Thank you for ordering our [*product or service name*]. As your account manager, I am writing to confirm that the [*product or service name*] you ordered has been [*received/installed/commenced*].

At [*your company name*], we understand that [*your company's general product benefit*] is vital to the success of your [*business or organization*]. If you have any further needs, please do not hesitate to contact me.

As you know, I am available at any time to help you with placing orders, discussing requirements, arranging product demonstrations or visits by you to us or vice versa. Do not hesitate to call me free of charge on [*toll-free number*].

For any other enquiries you may have, such as service calls and invoicing, call the following numbers:

Service calls	[*service number*]
Invoicing	[*customer administration number*]
Other queries	[*general number*]

Thank you once again. I look forward to being able to help you again in the near future.

Yours sincerely,

[*TAM name*]
Account manager

Note

Sending this letter reinforces the idea in customers' minds that you are concerned to ensure that they get the best from your company. Your company is clearly not the kind that likes to take the money and run. Research shows that it is just after a product has been bought that the customer is in need of most reinforcement. They are then most likely to have queries about the product, but may feel unclear about how to have them dealt with. Keep the dialogue going!

Not interested

> *Your company name*
> *Company address*
> *Toll-free telephone number*
> *Date*

Dear [*Salutation*],

Following our telephone conversation on [*date*], I should like to thank you for taking the time to talk to me.

Naturally, I am sorry you are not interested in our account management service, as it is designed to help you get the most out of our products and services.

Should you change your mind and wish to place any orders, discuss requirements or arrange product demonstrations, please do not hesitate to call me on [*toll-free number*].

I look forward to helping your business in the near future.

Yours sincerely,

[*TAM name*]
Account manager

Note

You need a standard letter for those customers who have been approached with the account management service and turned it down. You must leave the door open!

Not interested currently

> *Your company name*
> *Company address*
> *Toll-free telephone number*
> *Date*

Dear [*Salutation*],

Following our telephone conversation on [*date*], I should like to thank you for taking the time to talk to me.

The account management service we discussed is designed to help you get the most out of our products and services.

Although I was unable to help you during our recent discussion, I should like to remind you that I am your personal account manager should you wish to place any orders, discuss requirements or arrange product demonstrations. Please do not hesitate to call me on [*toll-free number*].

For any other enquiries you may have, such as service calls and invoicing, call the following numbers:

Service calls	[*service number*]
Invoicing	[*customer administration number*]
Other queries	[*general number*]

Meanwhile, as your account manager, I look forward to helping your business in the near future.

Yours sincerely,

[*TAM name*]
Account manager

Note

You need a standard letter for those customers who have been approached with the account management service and accepted the concept of account management but are not currently interested in buying any product or service from you. They will generally be happy to buy from you in the future. So, as before, the door must be left open for you to call them or them to call you.

Non-qualifiers for TAM service

> *Your company name*
> *Company address*
> *Toll-free telephone number*
> *Date*

Dear [*Salutation*],

Following out telephone conversation on [*date*], I should like to thank you for taking the time to talk to me.

Our discussion highlighted the fact that your company is one of our larger customers. As such, you will require a wide range of equipment and services and frequent calls by our sales force.

Therefore, I am passing your name on to [*name*], one of our field sales staff.

[*He/she*] is ideally suited to servicing your requirements and will from now on be your single point of contact for placing orders, discussing requirements, arranging product demonstrations or visits by you to us or vice versa. Do not hesitate to call [*him/her*] on [*toll-free number*].

For any other enquiries you may have, such as service calls and invoicing, please call the following numbers:

Service calls   [*service number*]
Invoicing   [*customer administration number*]
Other queries   [*general number*]

Thank you once again. [*Your company*] looks forward to being able to help you again in the near future.

Yours sincerely

TAM name
Account manager

Note

If you have just started telemanaging your customers, you will have discovered that many of your customers will be on the borderline between suitability for telemanagement and field sales management. You will discover this early on! The call guide for the first calls must be very sensitive, because it is guiding some customers through the advantages of being managed mainly over the telephone, with sales calls only when necessary. The option of remaining with a field sales person may be offered, or that of trialling the arrangement. If your customer survey has shown that, say, medium-sized customers feel neglected, then you are on fairly strong ground. However, you might just happen to have some good field sales staff who combined field and telemanaging roles. Substituting TAM for this will seem a bad deal for the customer, particularly if it means losing a good salesman.

In the end, however, if your company has decided that a particular category of customer must be telemanaged, you must present the facts to the customer, together with the evidence of success of the concept. Remember, if your product or service does require face-to-face calls, the customer will still receive them, but under telemanagement disciplines.

Product literature and quote request

> *Your company name*
> *Company address*
> *Toll-free telephone number*
> *Date*

Dear [*Salutation*],

Following our telephone conversation on [*date*], I should like to thank you for your interest in our [*product or service name*].

As you requested, I enclose a copy of our latest information on our [*product or service name*].

I also enclose an [*outline/firm*] quotation. This is based on current prices and valid for the next [*number*] days.

I shall call you again in a few days' time to confirm that you have received our information and to answer any questions you may have.

Naturally, if you prefer to talk to me before then, you can always reach me by calling free of charge on [*toll-free number*].

As you know, I am your personal account manager. My job is to help you in placing orders, discussing requirements, arranging product demonstrations or visits by you to us or vice versa.

For any other enquiries you may have, such as service calls and invoicing, call the following numbers:

Service calls   [*service number*]
Invoicing   [*customer administration number*]
Other queries   [*general number*]

Thank you once again for your request. I look forward to being able to help you again in the near future.

Yours sincerely,

[*TAM name*]
Account manager

Note

You need a standard letter to send out with all product or service literature and quotations. As every opportunity to reinforce the relationship should be taken, literature and quotations should *never* be sent out without a covering letter from the TAM. If letters are sent out from a central fulfilment house, the latter should hold all the TAM details to be inserted, plus the digitized signature. The other data should be taken from the literature request data.

Invitation to a sales seminar or showroom

> *Your company name*
> *Company address*
> *Toll-free telephone number*
> *Date*

Dear [*Salutation*],

Following our telephone conversation on [*date*], I should like to thank you for taking the time to discuss your needs with me. I confirm that I have arranged for a [*demonstration of (product)/sales visit concerning (product)/your visit to our showroom/seminar on (subject)*].

[*Select appropriate paragraph*].

The product demonstration will take place on [*date*] at [*time*] at [*location*]. I enclose details of how to get there. When you arrive, please contact [*name of TAM field sales staff or of demonstration manager*], who will be expecting you. After your visit, I shall give you a call to see whether you have any further questions.

[*or*] [*Name of TAM field sales staff*] will be coming to see you on [*date*] at [*time*] to discuss [*product or service*]. After [*he/she*] has been to see you, I shall give you a call to see whether you have any further questions.

[*or*] Your visit to our showroom has been set for [*date*] at [*time*]. I enclose details of how to get there. When you arrive, please contact [*name of TAM field sales staff or of demonstration manager*], who will be expecting you. After your visit, I shall give you a call to see whether you have any further questions.

[*or*] The seminar will take place on [*date*] at [*time*] at [*location*]. I enclose your invitation card and details of how to get there. When you arrive, please contact [*name of TAM field sales staff or of seminar manager*], who will be expecting you.

As you know, I am your personal account manager. My job is to help you in placing orders, discussing requirements, arranging product demonstrations or visits by you to us or vice versa. Do not hesitate to call me free of charge on [*toll-free number*].

For any other enquiries you may have, such as service calls and invoicing, please call the following numbers:

Service calls	[*service number*]
Invoicing	[*customer administration number*]
Other queries	[*general number*]

Thank you once again for your request. I look forward to being able to help you again in the near future.

Yours sincerely,

[*TAM name*]
Account manager

Note

Customers might wonder why the TAM is not going to be involved in face-to-face contact. The answer is that the TAM's place is to offer a telephone-based service. This must be explained to the customer during the call at which the contact is scheduled. Of course, the explanation should be in terms of meeting the needs of all TAM customers, rather than in terms of selling.

Customer moving within TAM area

> *Your customer name*
> *Company address*
> *Toll-free number*
> *Date*

Dear [*Salutation*],

Following our telephone conversation on [*date*], I should like to thank you for taking the time to talk to me.

From our discussion, I understand that your company will be moving in [*number*] weeks' time.

As your account manager, I am here to help you in placing orders, discussing requirements, arranging product demonstrations or visits by you to us or vice versa. I shall be pleased to answer any questions you may have and to help you with any special requirements you may have for our products and services as a result of your move.

As agreed, I shall be contacting you [*number*] days before you move, to discuss your needs.

Naturally, if you prefer to talk to me before then, you can always reach me by calling free of charge on [*toll-free number*].

For any other enquiries you may have, such as service calls and invoicing, please call the following numbers:

Service calls   [*service number*]
Invoicing   [*customer administration number*]
Other queries   [*general number*]

Thank you once again for your request. I look forward to being able to help you again in the near future.

Your sincerely,

[*TAM name*]
Account manager

Note

If you are using TAM to manage your relationship with smaller businesses, you will know that these businesses move quite often. If your product or service is the kind that requires changing when a company moves, then your customers will need you during and after the move. This is a friendly way of cementing the relationship. It is particularly important to do this as far in advance as possible. This is because when a company moves, it is likely to contact new suppliers and perhaps dispose of existing equipment.

113

Customer moving to another TAM area

> *Your company name*
> *Company address*
> *Toll-free telephone number*
> *Date*

Dear [*Salutation*],

Following our telephone conversation on [*date*], I should like to thank you for taking the time to talk to me.

From our discussion, I understand that your company will be moving to another location in [*number*] weeks' time.

I have notified [*name of TAM in new area*], who will be your new account manager and single point of contact for placing orders, discussing requirements, arranging product demonstrations or visits by you to us or vice versa. [*New TAM first name*] will be pleased to answer any questions you may have and to help you with any special requirements you may have for our products and services as a result of your move.

Naturally, if you prefer to talk to me before then, you can always reach me by calling free of charge on [*toll-free number*].

For any other enquiries you may have, such as service calls and invoicing, call the following numbers:

Service calls   [*service number*]
Invoicing   [*customer administration number*]
Other queries   [*general number*]

Your contact numbers in your new location will be toll free to your new account manager

Service calls   [*service number*]
Invoicing   [*customer administration number*]
Other queries   [*general number*]

Thank you once again for your request. I look forward to being able to help you again in the near future.

Yours sincerely,

[*TAM name*]
Account manager

Note

Small businesses may move between your sales areas, so you need to transfer account management smoothly. This letter tells the customer what the new arrangements are, but also offers help during the transition. This prevents the customer falling 'between the planks' at what may be a critical time for your relationship with him.

12

Planning campaigns

The TAM relationship with customers is a true account management relationship. The customer's needs are paramount. The TAM succeeds to the extent that customer needs are satisfied properly.

However, the TAM is only one part of the sales and marketing organization which results in products being marketed and sold. The TAM operation will not always have complete freedom as to which products to sell. That would be splendid in theory, but in practice, in most companies, it would be impossible. Like any other sales channel, the TAM operation will be targeted to sell certain amounts of different products. The successful account manager lives with this pressure, and should not deal with it by forcing products on unwilling customers. TAMs sell by identifying customer needs. This leads to the TAM determining customer needs for the product the TAM is targeted to sell. With a large customer base to choose from, the discerning TAM spends time trying to identify which customers are good prospects for particular products before asking them if they are interested. Figure 12.1 illustrates how telemanagement can be initiated through a series of campaigns.

If your company has a proper database marketing system, then when a product campaign is being planned, the product marketers or brand managers doing the planning should have analysed the customers on the database to identify which represent the best prospects for the product in question. Having done this, they should have reached conclusions as to the characteristics of good prospects. These should then be transformed into selection criteria for a marketing campaign – whether direct mail or a TAM call or both. The media they choose to target the best prospects should be chosen on the basis of past performance with the customer group in question.

In a truly marketing-oriented company, the need for the campaign (and ideally for the product) would not be agreed until the market had been shown to exist and be selectable from the database! However, we know that in reality this situation is rarely reached. At a minimum, however, some testing should have taken place.

Like all marketing campaigns, a good TAM campaign takes time to plan. Once the timing and targeting for the campaign has been agreed, the nature of the offer to be made to TAM customers must be determined, and the creative (the call guide) designed. In addition, close co-ordination with other marketing efforts should be achieved. For example, there

115

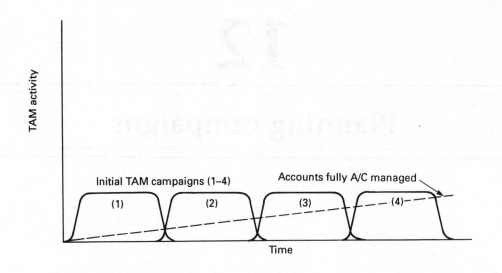

Figure 12.1 TAM customer contact

may be a mailing to all database customers who fit the selection criteria, irrespective of the channel through which they are managed. This mailing should ideally be customized to each channel. TAM customers should therefore receive the letter from their TAM, not from a central marketing manager. If this proves impossible, because of co-ordination problems, at the very least the TAM should be informed exactly when the letter is being sent out, so that at an appropriate interval, the TAM can call and see how (and whether!) the communication has been received.

A good TAM campaign can take two to three months to prepare, including the time for call-guide development and testing. Trying to mount a campaign at too short notice almost invariably leads to problems of quality. This is one good reason why TAM campaign planning should be an integral part of marketing planning. It should not be left until after the marketing plan has been published. Integration will make much more time available for preparation of letters and call guides, and will enable more accurate work to be done on targeting.

The relationship between campaign planning and marketing planning is, however, not a simple one-way flow. In the process of campaign planning, you are bound to discover that some of your marketing plans were wrong. You may discover that some marketing objectives were too tough, others too low. You may find that for some markets, telemanaging can play a greater part than you realized, in others that its effectiveness is lower than you thought.

If you feel that the relationship between marketing planning and TAM campaign planning has not been properly thought through in your business, you must raise it as an important issue. Leading users of direct marketing approaches such as TAM have fully integrated the two approaches. In these companies, from the moment marketing objectives and strategies are conceived, the campaigns required to implement them are also conceived and the right media and channels for communicating with and selling to customers are also identified. In these companies, marketing objectives and strategies are determined in the light of past campaign results.

Without this approach, you are bound to end up trying to use direct marketing to do the wrong things some of the time.

A word of warning

If your company runs its marketing primarily through campaigns, there is a danger that these campaigns will be allowed to dominate the TAM operation. This might lead to a TAM operation failing, because it is forced to behave like a 'foot in the door' sales force. This must be avoided. A TAM operation can be very effectively 'kick-started' through a series of campaigns. But after three or four successful campaigns, the TAMs will be working to customers' buying cycles, not your company's sales cycles. Company-driven sales campaigns can still be run through a mature TAM operation, but only against the background of true account management. The best analogy is that a campaign should be like 'this month's special offer', made only to customers who TAMs believe will benefit from it. All that is written about campaigns here and in Chapter 13 should be read with this caveat in mind.

The campaign process

In principle, the process of developing and implementing a TAM campaign should run through the following sequences:

- *Planning* – deciding how you are going to meet your marketing objectives through one or more campaigns, with specific objectives, target markets, promoting specific products and services, at particular times.
- *Development* – when you determine the details of each campaign.

- *Implementation* – when you run each campaign.
- *Evaluation* – when you analyse the results of each campaign.

Campaign planning

Ideally, your marketing plan gives you clear objectives, strategies and targets. As we stressed above, these should have been specified taking into account your TAM capability. You are now concerned with translating the marketing plan into actions. For this reason, we recommend that as soon as possible, your TAM campaign intentions are summarized in the form of an *outline brief*. This document is effectively a summary of your intentions – what you want to promote, when, to whom and how. In response to the marketing plan, you should produce a series of outline briefs, and summarize them in the form of an overall plan of TAM campaigns. Of course, you will also need campaigns to deal with unexpected problems or opportunities, but these tactical campaigns demand just as professional an approach as the more strategic campaigns.

Why is it not appropriate just to produce a list of likely campaigns, before going into the details of outline briefs? In our view, writing the outline brief ensures that you know exactly what you are planning to do. Without it, you will not know with which other campaigns your campaign will clash. Therefore, you will not have a strong basis for determining campaign timings.

Obviously, the outline brief is refined and added to as the time for initiation of more detailed work on each campaign approaches. But by preparing the outline brief early, and by circulating it to all parties involved, you will ensure that clashes, data problems and resource bottlenecks are minimized and co-operation maximized.

117

Drawing up and, where necessary, getting agreement to the outline brief must be done as early as competitive and market conditions allow. The brief is the key to well-planned and co-ordinated campaigns. It summarizes the main details of the campaign. It has the additional benefits that it:

- helps you organize your thinking
- gives top-line guidance to implementers
- communicates the campaign internally and to suppliers; if your call guides are developed by an external supplier (e.g. telemarketing agency), they will need briefing in this way.
- is the supporting document for more detailed forms covering different aspects of the campaign (e.g. fulfilment procedures)

Campaign development

Campaign development is when you put together all the details of the campaign (detailed targeting – enclosing lists, timing, offer, call guides, etc.). In this period, your main concern is with getting all the details of the campaign right. This will ensure it runs smoothly once it is launched. Campaign development is given further detailed consideration below.

Campaign implementation

When the campaign actually runs, a major concern is likely to be ensuring that the logistics are running smoothly (e.g. calls being made on time, responses being handled and fulfilled) and that interim results are analysed to see whether any campaign details need modifying.

Campaign evaluation

After the campaign has run, you want to find out what worked and what did not. Here, the prime activity is analysis of results by different categories (business sector, state of existing relationship etc.).

We have already seen what it takes to implement each TAM campaign, and how results are evaluated. We now focus on campaign development.

Campaign development

We live in the age of integrated communication. Our aim is to deploy *all marketing communications media* together, in an integrated fashion. Mail and telephone work best when they are deployed in this way. For example, if you want to create national awareness for a new product and then find customers for it, media advertising followed by direct mail and then a TAM call may be the best way. For these media to work well they must be planned and executed together. Because they are traditionally planned separately, special attention must be given to project managing them together. In doing this, you must be prepared to integrate the different concepts which are traditionally the preserve of discrete marketing disciplines. The 'proposition' and 'key thought' used in the advertising campaign must be transferred to the TAM call for the two to work well together. In this way, the right 'take-out' and consumer action will be achieved.

The TAM concept of the managed dialogue must be applied to media advertising. This becomes the 'front end' of the contact cycle, and may indeed spur a telemanaged customer to call his TAM.

Targeting

Consumer targeting

Targeting must be as specific as possible. With a clear statement of marketing objectives and strategies, you should be able to identify the main customer types who form the target market for the campaign. Good customer targeting is a creative process, split into two separate and very different issues:

- who you are aiming your campaign at
- how to find them and gain access to them

Creativity is required in answering the 'who' question, to determine the different customer types who fit into our target market definition. At this stage, you try to (almost) forget such critical issues as whether you can actually identify these people. Instead, you use your knowledge of your customers to build a picture of the different types of person who form your target market. For example, the target market for a very high-contribution executive pension plan might include directors of very profitable small businesses, or directors of big companies. Your database should give you the ability to turn each of these definitions into different selections. Once you know that you can select these different types of customer, you can allocate resource to developing different, relevant promotional actions for each customer type.

You should be able to target much more accurately after you implement telemanagement, because of the depth of the data that you will acquire through TAM's needs analysis work.

Segment size

The *number* of customers in the target market – and hence the number of contact records opened for the TAMs – should be determined by your quantified campaign objectives. In some cases, you may be targeting *all* customers in a particular geographical market who fit a particular definition. In other cases, you should have quantified sales objectives, which should lead through expected response and sales rates to a target number to be contacted. If the number to be sold by your campaign is critical, but you have no idea of response or final sales rates, then – if you have time – a test is indicated. Once again, a properly integrated marketing and campaign planning framework is a critical factor in making time for testing.

You should also consider the size of the target segment in relation to the amount of time TAMs have available to call. This may depend upon the priorities you assign to different campaigns.

Contact strategy

The fine tuning of targeting leads naturally to the question of contact strategy and media choice. At this stage, forget the detail. What you are trying to do is to offer different and creative ways for the individual to receive information and respond to you. You may want to invite your customers to call your TAMs. You might want to use a questionnaire as a second step in your contact strategy, to help you fine tune the next step.

Timing

Timing can be split into two elements:

Macro-timing

This covers when the campaign should be run. It takes into account other campaigns you might be running and the target customers' needs.

The macro-timing is determined by your marketing planning work, which should lead to a co-ordinated series of campaigns. Obviously, a key part of the justification for any campaign is why it should run at the proposed time.

You should make sure that your calling frequency does not rise too high. Obviously, every call the TAM makes must be good quality, relevant and consistent with other contacts. No calls must be idle. They must all be of benefit to both caller and respondent. If you have no policy on frequency, you should develop one and keep it under review in the light of experience.

Micro-timing

This covers when each element of the campaign's contact strategy should be run. It takes into account the timing of other elements of the campaign and what you know about the likely receptiveness of customers at different times (of day, week etc.).

Micro-timing should be based on in-depth knowledge of customers' receptiveness to different types of communication and your TAMs' knowledge of how their customers respond to different types of communication (letters, brochures, calls).

Do not forget the usual direct marketing timing issues, for example

- avoiding times when customers' attention is elsewhere (e.g. in consumer markets, immediately pre-Christmas), and focusing on times when attention guaranteed (e.g. post-Christmas)
- ensuring that the merchandise is ready to go out and able to be delivered

The offer

The offer is not just a description of the product. It combines one or more propositions with incentive(s) to try the proposition. More than one proposition may be promoted in a campaign.

The areas to explore for propositions include:

- product characteristics – performance, quality of service, reliability, variety of functions
- market factors – types of customer, market share, exclusivity
- ways of using the product – to save time, to make more profit, to treat yourself
- surprising facts about the product, users or usage (used by celebrities)
- price characteristics – value for money, money-back guarantee, discounts
- image – top quality, good value, friendly, reliable
- needs-satisfying – physical, status etc.
- company – nationality, energy, direction, customer-orientation
- disadvantages of non-use – what you lose or miss by not buying
- competitive comparison – product, company
- newsworthy – recent changes, anniversaries, topical events, new facilities

All these propositions will be weak unless the customer is given a reason to respond and a date to respond by. Even within a TAM relationship, you will find that a strong offer works better than a weak one (e.g. with no close date). However, too much propositioning of customers with offers may cause problems, so strong offers should be deployed carefully. In telemanagement, the offer must be tailored to previous discussion between TAM and customer concerning the product or service in question, for example relevant to:

- specific departments that would find it useful, *now*
- specific business aims of the customer that are top priority, *now*
- the customer's budget cycle, making *now* a good time to buy

Creative

In all forms of marketing communication, the creative element, for example the expression of the campaign in words (printed, broadcast or in call guides), is always the most obvious and attracts the most interest from management. Despite this, and the apparent claim that it is not hard to get the creative right, poor creative is still a major contributory factor to delayed campaigns and last-minute rushes.

The brief is critical to good creative. Omissions which are particularly likely to cause problems with call guides include:

- imprecise or too generalized a description of the target market
- inadequate specification of how the buying process takes place
- lack of clarity on desired tone, proposition, and branding
- inclusion of too many objectives
- inconsistency of message and tone with the TAMs role

Promotional contacts

The promotional actions you use for your campaign should be as simple as possible, and based on what you *know* works for customers in the target market. However, you should normally test any new approach, otherwise you will never give yourself the chance to learn.

Whatever promotional actions you choose, make sure that you know the objectives and expected results of each step. This will ensure that everyone involved in your campaign knows exactly what to do or expect, before the campaign runs.

For each action step, specify:

- The objectives – what you want to happen to customers who are the target of the campaign (e.g. be informed or persuaded, give information, identify themselves as being in the target market – i.e. hand-raising, buy a product).
- How you want them to respond (e.g. fill in a questionnaire and send it, buy a product and give proof of purchase).
- How the promotional action will achieve this (e.g. description of TAM call or brochure).
- How many you expect to respond in different ways.

Ideally, try to achieve your result in one call for each target segment.

Narrowing down options

When you have drafted out your campaign, in terms of target segments and promotional actions, you may find you have identified too many possibilities. Following them all can lead to high promotional costs and poor results. At this stage, ask yourself the following questions:

- Do you need all the target segments you have identified?
- If so, do you need to address them simultaneously? Is there scope for prioritizing or for seeing whether the most important segments produce the right level of response?
- Are there economies in combining segments?

Getting the numbers right

Unless you can show you are making a profit from your activity, your use of TAM will be at risk. For this reason, you should usually try to defray the costs of developing TAM over as large a target as possible.

Try to identify the rates of trade-off you are getting between sales rates and market coverage. Too high revenues per call may mean that you have too small an operation, which is effectively creaming the market. If the opposite occurs, your operation may be too large. This also applies to individual campaigns within the TAM operation.

The process for determining campaign size should go as follows:

1 *Segment* – Break down your target market into target segments
2 *Costs and benefits* – Identify the likely cost and benefits of promoting to each target segment. Distinguish fixed costs from variable costs, and also what the effect of more precise targeting and more targeted offer design will have on response rates. In some cases, where a clear benefit cannot be stated in profit terms but where the promotion is considered essential for strategic reasons, you may want to use what is called an 'alternative cost' measure. This measures what it would have cost you to promote to the customer using the next best method.
3 *Lists* – If you have research which indicates that large numbers of your target market are not on your TAM or main database, consult with your database administration about which lists to use and how to get them on your database. This might be the case if many of your customers bought indirectly, or if past sales records were low quality.
4 *Database analysis* – If large numbers of your target market are on your database,

experiment with selections until you are sure that either:

- you have identified a number of target segments which are not overlapping and which differ significantly in the kind of offer that can be made to them, or that
- a simple selection criterion will suffice, because more complex selection criteria do not give you target segments of sufficient size for you to cost-effectively and meaningfully promote to

5 *Selections* – Define your segments for selection purposes.
6 *Measurement* – Make sure that you specify all the criteria by which you will be measuring the success of your campaign, at each stage of your contact strategy.

Testing

In telemanagement, the best route to success is to find what works and to go on using it, but you must test to see whether you could have done better. You need also to confine your testing to the areas where you believe the greatest return lies.

If your TAM operation is of a reasonable size, in terms of number of customers covered (say over 20 000), there is ample scope for testing offers and call guides. In all campaign briefs, there should be a clear specification of what is being tested, and what you want to learn by testing.

Your ability to test is limited by the fact that the expected sales result, size of test sample, significance level (the probability that our estimate is accurate) and confidence interval (the definition of the upper and lower limits of our estimate) are related. For example, suppose we are planning a campaign where we expect the sales rate to be 4 per cent. If we want to be 95 per cent sure whether the result, if applied to the whole target market, will fall within the confidence interval of between 3–5 percent, the sample size needs to be much larger than if we only want to be 90 per cent sure that the result falls within the band 2–6 per cent. What size you choose depends upon the costs and benefits of the campaign. For example, if break-even is 1.5 per cent, you may be happier with the second set of criteria, and so be happier with a smaller test cell.

In a TAM operation, test results must be interpreted with caution. This is because the sale may take some time to be realized, perhaps a long time after the test campaign has been closed. It might be that the customer temporarily deferred the idea, but came back to it later, stimulated by the TAM. If the test is of a comprehensive campaign, supporting several sales channels (of which the TAM is just one), should the eventual sale be credited to the TAM or the campaign? The simple answer to this question is – both! The result may show that the campaign was most effective when run in a TAM environment.

13

Running campaigns

Whether one TAM in one office, or a hundred or more spread over countries or continents, the TAM operation must be run properly. We have explained already how to set the TAM operation up and how to make sure it is run effectively. There is however an additional dimension – quality.

A TAM operation normally runs as a series of campaigns to sell products and services. This is interwoven with a regular calling cycle which develops needs across the portfolio and takes advantage of changes and developments on the customer's side, to sell a wide range of products. Although we might want to be indifferent as to which products and services customers order, we can rarely afford this luxury. We have factories to keep running, inventories to sell, and service staff to keep busy. If we do our marketing well, what we want to sell should coincide with what we want customers to buy. But we still need to organize our efforts in campaigns. We do this to get the benefits of marketing focus. These include:

- availability of inventory
- preparedness of service staff
- motivation of sales staff
- support from national marketing communications

Campaigns do well in marketing because they work on the principal of concentration, domination and repetition. In a properly orchestrated campaign, the messages from national direct mailings, advertising, PR and from the TAM are all co-ordinated in terms of content and timing. Customers are more likely to respond positively to TAM calls in these circumstances.

Campaigns can go wrong, however. In a well-managed campaign, everything happens when it is supposed to. This is because

- it has been fully and properly planned, in time
- everyone involved in it knows what they should be doing, and when
- there are safety checks – if something looks like slipping, either additional support is provided or the campaign is formally slipped and rescheduled.

Unfortunately, many marketing and sales campaigns are not well planned and managed. This is often because no-one has thought through the information requirements of good planning, or implemented a process for providing information support to the planning process. Therefore, we now outline the kind of process you might adopt for planning campaigns for telemanaged customers. Given the constraints of space, we have depicted in detail one

125

particular process model, but you should find it easy to adopt it to your own requirements.

Campaign process details

We will consider what we believe should happen at each stage in the campaign process and who should do it. To do this, we need to refer to the information provided in some detail. Our approach has therefore been to organize the information required during a campaign into a number of forms. These should be completed as the campaign planning progresses. How you use this is up to you. We believe that without properly documented campaign files, you are likely to commit more errors of commission and omission than otherwise. With the information properly organized, you will at least have the basis for quality. Remember, the quality of every contact between a TAM customer and your company can strengthen or weaken the relationship and its power to produce sales.

The forms themselves are illustrated on pages 130–63 and each form is followed by detailed explanatory notes.

1 *Campaign definition and accountabilities* – describing the requirement in brief and saying who is involved in delivering it.

2 *Campaign coverage* – objectives, strategies, and target markets, and where the campaign fits in overall marketing and promotional strategy.

3 *Campaign detail* – what responses are required, measurement criteria, what exactly is being promoted, what its features and benefits are, and competitive issues.

4 *Campaign elements* – what are the detailed requirements of the campaign.

5 *Initial estimates* – what you think the campaign is going to cost and what revenue you expect.

6 *Management and media timing plans* – the main milestones in campaign planning.

7 *Mail and TAM timing plans* – the main milestones for direct mail and TAM actions.

8 *List selection brief* – which specific customers you want to target.

9 *Contact and fulfilment strategy* – what you're going to do with each group of customers you target.

10 *Contact strategy diagrams* – a diagrammatic representation of (14) and (15).

11 *Selection feedback report* – how many customers have been selected by your selection criteria.

12 *Outbound TAM calling* – detailed brief to TAM operations for outbound calling.

13 *Inbound TAM calling* – as (12), but for inbound.

14 *Questionnaire summary* – to record details of questions asked in telemarketing or mailshots.

15 *Fulfilment pack summary* – details of contents and suppliers.

16 *Fulfilment letter summary* – details of letter.

17 *Print production and distribution* – handling of printed items.

18 *Sales and service delivery* – so other units involved in the sales and service delivery cycle are properly briefed.

Process

1 As early as possible, the person initiating the campaign works

outs its main lines, completing as much of *Forms 1 to 5* as possible, ideally after discussion with the senior manager responsible for TAMs.

2 When he is ready, the initiator submits these forms through your TAM campaign co-ordination process. The manager responsible for co-ordination checks what other campaigns are planned, and also checks the details of the submission. The campaign is agreed (or not). Provisional plans *(Forms 6 and 7)* are agreed.

3 If the campaign is approved, *Forms 1 to 4* are submitted as a brief to the group or agency writing call guides and to those responsible for any direct mail strategy and copy. As part of their response, timing plans are confirmed.

4 Your people (and/or suppliers) work out the right targeting, timing, offer and creative for your campaign. You firm up on selections *(Form 8)* and document the contact strategy and media *(Forms 9 and 10)*

5 The systems people tell you how many customers your selection criteria have selected *(Form 11)*. You revise your criteria if necessary.

6 You brief your TAM operation *(Forms 12 and 13)*.

7 You make sure that all the questions used in TAM calling and mailshot are properly recorded, so that systems staff know how to handle them *(Form 15)*.

8 You determine and record your fulfilment pack and letter details *(Forms 15 and 16)*, and how you want print produced and distributed *(Form 17)*.

9 You ensure that all other sales and service delivery communications are received, understood and agreed (Form 18).

10 Your campaign goes live.

Campaign administration

The above may seem a rather complex set of actions, but it represents what goes on in most companies – albeit often verbally or informally on the back of an envelope. All that we have done is to rationalize it. If you implement such a process, you must work to a clear set of administrative procedures. Here is our suggestion.

1 A master file must be maintained by the person given responsibility for campaign administration.

2 The file physically documents the process, but the process itself consists of management decision and action, followed by documentation.

3 The files must be properly packaged, with clearly marked sections, so absence or incompleteness of any form can be detected.

4 Some forms will be completed gradually, often as part of the response to an earlier stage of briefing. According to how you organize yourself, certain items of information should be mandatory by certain stages.

5 Each form has one or more 'principal recipients', but will be copied to all the team. All will have a copy of the file and its contents, updated each time a change is made.

6 Whenever a change or addition is made, this is an amendment. The relevant sheet should be issued with revised date.

7 The summary of the response to each brief (where appropriate) is also kept on file. Suppliers must produce simple summaries for this purpose (no more than one page).

8 As outputs of the earlier part of the process emerge (e.g. draft copy, graphics), they must be circulated to all suppliers by each supplier.

There are obvious benefits in computerizing such a process. Without this, running the process will be very cumbersome. In particular, reporting will be very slow and paper-intense. The kind of reports that will need to be issued include the following:

- projects at different statuses
- date each form was last updated
- milestones due and missed
- budgets allocated
- quotes accepted
- data missing
- results summary
- work loading on staff

Individual campaign reports should be filed with the campaign documentation. Many reports will be across-campaign, and may be the subject for departmental review meetings. Reports can also be used to track the performance of particular suppliers, brand or product managers, and direct marketing staff.

The forms

The forms provided here serve three purposes:

- *To help plan and implement your campaign.* The forms help you do this by ensuring that you cover the detail that a TAM campaign typically requires.
- *To provide a basis for formally briefing others.* If you work out the detail; correctly, and use the form to make a record of it, then you have created a clear basis for communicating your intentions to others on the team. The very act of planning creates the campaign file.
- *To communicate your plans clearly.* Apart from those on the campaign team, others need to know what you are planning. Creation of a master file using these forms makes this easier to do.

These forms may seem rather bureaucratic. However, all the information they cover has to be written down some-

where, and communicated to someone. The forms merely provide a systematic way of ensuring that all planning, briefing and communication actions are carried out. Our experience is that unless you specify all the details of a campaign, you are very likely to have something go wrong. Nearly all the forms constitute either a brief or a response to a brief. The later the order of the form, the further downstream in the campaign development process it is used to brief or respond. For example, the later forms brief fulfilment houses, call guide writers and printers.

There is not a rigidly fixed sequence to the completion of the forms, as some may be completed in anticipation. If your company is weak at planning, you may find that at first you end up completing the later forms before the earlier ones! However, in principle, the order should be roughly as presented.

The responsibility for completing each form is likely to vary according to how your company is organized. In some companies, the responsibility for all the forms might be best allocated to the senior manager responsible for the TAM operation. In others, it might be a specialist direct marketer. In yet others, perhaps less centralized, a product manager may be responsible for the earlier forms, and a direct marketing assistant for later forms. What you need to make sure is that *every* form has a defined person responsible for its completion, and that there is *one* person responsible for maintenance of the master file.

You may not need to use every form, or every section of each form, for every campaign. Some sections may be irrelevant for your campaign. You may need to modify some of these forms to suit your purpose.

Ideally, the form should be compute-rized. This not only makes it easier to complete them, but also allows us to analyse the data in the forms. However you computerize them, we recommend that you first customize them and then trial them extensively on paper.

The recipients of copies of the form are determined by the details on Form 1, which shows accountabilities.

Filling in the forms

Entry on all the forms

The following four entries are made at the top of each form:

Campaign title: The formal name of the campaign, e.g. small business campaign for product X, customer loyalty campaign for Spring 1992.
Campaign code: This would be your company campaign code. It is essential that you determine a permanent system for campaign coding. This will be the coding that you use on your main customer database system to refer to the campaign.
Originator: This is the name of the person who completes the form in question. Who this is will be determined by how your company allocates responsibility for initiating and managing campaigns.
Date of issue: This is when the last version of this form was issued. As a campaign evolves, it is likely to go through many changes. If the campaign team starts to operate from different versions of the same form, disaster could strike. You may therefore wish to create a separate form, showing when each form was last updated, and circulate it with the campaign documentation.

Where additional material is needed to provide justification or support to the information on any form, it should always be attached. The forms aim to force communication and precision, but cannot substitute for the much greater volume of information needed to brief suppliers and manage campaigns through.

Then follows the campaign description.

Form 1: Campaign definition and accountabilities

CAMPAIGN NAME_____ CODE_____

ORIGINATOR_____ DATE OF ISSUE_____

DESCRIPTION OF REQUIREMENT_____
_____
_____

PLANNED CALL START DATE_____ PLANNED CALL END DATE_____

CAMPAIGN MANAGER_____

SUPPLIERS

COMPANY   CONTACT NAME   OBJECTIVE/ROLE OF COMPANY ON CAMPAIGN

1._____ _____ _____

2._____ _____ _____

3._____ _____ _____

4._____ _____ _____

5._____ _____ _____

TAM OPERATION INVOLVEMENT

OPERATION   TYPE OF INVOLVEMENT

1._____ _____

2._____ _____

3._____ _____

4._____ _____

5._____ _____

6._____ _____

7._____ _____

8._____ _____

9._____ _____

10._____ _____

OTHERS ON CIRCULATION LIST FOR ALL CAMPAIGN DOCUMENTATION
(keep to minimum)

NAME   REASON FOR INVOLVEMENT

_____ _____

_____ _____

Notes

Description of requirement gives a brief description of the campaign (but fuller than the name!). It should include statements on size, target market, and offer, and refer to any wider campaign of which it is part. Thus, our campaign above, loyalty campaign for Spring 1992 might be described as: 'Campaign to raise the loyalty of all TAM customers to our entire product range, as part of our competitive defence strategy'.

Planned call start and call end dates gives the start and end dates of TAM calling.

Campaign manager is the person formally responsible for delivering the campaign. Who this is depends on how you organize your marketing, as discussed above.

Suppliers give the company name, contact name and objective or role of company on the campaign, for each supplier. This is the basis for mailing all documentation and reports, as well as identifying the complete campaign team. As further suppliers are involved, it will need to be updated, by the campaign manager.

Objective/role of company/dept on campaign gives the role of each supplier on the campaign, and has the same status as the above entry. This list will be added to as the campaign develops. An example of an entry would be 'handling of coupon responses'.

TAM operation involvement states which TAM operations will be involved, and what type of involvement they may have. This is for large companies with several TAM operations. For example, one operation might be involved in a test and the full campaign, one for a limited range of products, and so on.

Others on circulation list for all campaign documentation will be added to as necessary by the campaign manager.

Form 2: Campaign coverage

CAMPAIGN NAME_____CODE_____

ORIGINATOR_____DATE OF ISSUE_____

TEST OR ROLL-OUT_____

AIM OF TEST_____

IF TEST, ROLL-OUT STRATEGY_____

_____

OBJECTIVES OF MARKETING STRATEGY OF WHICH CAMPAIGN FORMS PART

1._____

2._____

3._____

MAIN ELEMENTS OF OVERALL MARKETING STRATEGY

1._____

2._____

3._____

OBJECTIVES OF TAM CAMPAIGN

1._____

2._____

3._____

REQUIRED CONSISTENCY WITH OTHER CAMPAIGNS AND ACTIVITIES

1._____

2._____

3._____

PROPOSITION (key issue/offer from prospect's point of view)

_____

_____

PREVIOUS PROMOTIONAL ACTIVITY TARGETED AT THE SAME AUDIENCE_____

_____

TARGET MARKETS (customer types)

1._____

2._____

Notes

This form summarizes campaign objectives and strategy and testing issues. The information is needed by those developing the creative and campaign strategy and also determines campaign priorities.

Objectives are the 'what', and strategies the 'how'. Thus, to achieve the objective of more profit, the strategy of relaunching a product may be chosen. The TAM objective might be to support the relaunch, by, for example, achieving particular levels of awareness, volume of enquiries and/or actual sales. The strategies might be to target TAM calls to identify potential new users within existing accounts, or to cross-sell to users of another of the company's products. Objectives should always be quantified, so that we know whether the campaign is likely to be a good investment (and afterwards, whether it was).

Test or roll-out is whether the campaign is a test or a final programme.

If test, roll-out strategy: If the campaign is a test, then this states what will be done with the result. There are several kinds of test. You may be testing whether the target market offers the right response. Or you may be testing which market is the best. Or the target market may be given, and you want to find the best offer for it. For a test of the offer, the statement might be 'Test mail followed by TAM call followed by pack, roll out one which produces best response'. If the test is of targeting, the statement might be 'Test in target market. If very successful, roll-out within 6 months, if borderline, modify and re-test, if very unsuccessful,

scrap'. Each of these criteria (e.g. very successful, borderline) should be defined.

Objectives of marketing strategy of which campaign forms part: should provide the objectives and strategy for all campaigns. These should be quantifiable and quantified.

Main elements of overall marketing strategy: should cover the marketing strategies which your company's marketers are planning to use to achieve their objectives. TAM will only be one part of this for most companies.

Objectives of TAM campaign: are based on your assessment of the contribution that the TAM campaign can make to achieving the marketing objectives.

Required consistency with other campaigns and activities: indicates how far the campaign must fit creatively with other campaigns targeted at the same audience, and how far it should use ideas employed by other types of marketing communication targeted at TAM customers (e.g. advertising). Timing issues should also be mentioned (e.g. avoid proximity to promotion of Product Y).

Proposition is the key issue/offer from the prospect's point of view. An example would be 'Try our product X before (date) and you will find that it makes doing Y a lot more pleasant'.

Previous promotional activity: If the customers targeted for this campaign have been the target of other product campaigns recently, these should be specified, to ensure consistency and avoid clashes in messages.

Target markets (customer types) states what sort of customers we are aiming the campaign at.

Form 3: Campaign detail

CAMPAIGN NAME_____CODE_____

ORIGINATOR_____DATE OF ISSUE_____

DESIRED CUSTOMER RESPONSE

1._____

2._____

3._____

MEASUREMENT CRITERIA

1._____

2._____

3._____

4._____

PRODUCTS/SERVICES/PROGRAMMES TO BE PROMOTED/OFFERED   CODE

1._____   _____

2._____   _____

3._____   _____

4._____   _____

PRODUCT OR PROGRAMME ATTRIBUTES

PRODUCT/SERVICE/PROGRAMME 1

PRICE_____

FEATURES_____

_____

BENEFITS_____

_____

POSITION RELATIVE TO SIMILAR PRODUCTS/SERVICES/PROGRAMMES IN PORTFOLIO

_____

and so on for each product/service/programme

DIRECT COMPETITION

COMPANY	PRODUCT	COMMENT (e.g. SW/OT vs your offering)
_____	_____	_____
_____	_____	_____
_____	_____	_____

Notes

Desired customer response: is what we want the customer either to take out from the campaign or to do. It should be tied to measurement criteria. Examples include: to visit showroom, to sample product Y, to buy service X.

Measurement criteria: are the criteria by which you will measure the success of the campaign.

Products/services/programmes to be promoted: lists what you are promoting. If you have a coding system, then the code should be entered. It may be used to tie budgetary requirements together. Your customer database system will also need the codes (e.g. for lead handling and reporting). Where the product range being promoted is very broad, the codes for the main products should be entered. You may also have market sector or segment codes, if your marketing is specialized along these lines.

Product or programme attributes: For each product of programme, you should specify the main details, as follows:

- *Price* the product is offered at. For programmes not involving the sale of a product, this will not apply, unless an entry price or subscription is charged.
- *Features* applies to products and programmes. Main features only should be listed (e.g. a product's functions and performance parameters, the description of what the customer sees in a programme, such as a newsletter).
- *Benefits* of how the product or programme will meet the objectives of target customers, expressed in customer language.
- *Position relative to similar products in portfolio*: Where there are similar products, TAMs, call guide and mailshot writers must position this product relative to others.

Direct competition

This helps TAMs, call guide and mailshot writers understand what they have to pitch their campaign against.

- *Companies*: Main competitive companies for the specific product, in order of competitiveness.
- *Products*: Names of their main products.
- *Comment*: A brief comparison of the product with your offering (strengths, weaknesses, opportunities, threats) and will give the agency a clue about the main competitive angle to be taken. You are likely to need more space here, but a summary never hurts (e.g. 'pricey but high quality', 'cheap and cheerful').

Form 4: Campaign elements

CAMPAIGN NAME_____CODE_____

ORIGINATOR_____DATE OF ISSUE_____

	Y/N	IMPLEMENTER	SUPPLIER CO.	SUPPLIER CONTACT	BUDGET
PROCESSES					
LIST SELECTION	___	_____	_____	_____	_____
LIST CLEANING	___	_____	_____	_____	_____
DATA CAPTURE	___	_____	_____	_____	_____
CH I/B PRESS	___	_____	_____	_____	_____
TAM MAIL	___	_____	_____	_____	_____
CH I/B MAIL	___	_____	_____	_____	_____
TAM O/B	___	_____	_____	_____	_____
MAILING DESIGN	___	_____	_____	_____	_____
O/B POSTAGE	___	_____	_____	_____	_____
FULFIL POSTAGE	___	_____	_____	_____	_____
LIST FOR EVENT	___	_____	_____	_____	_____

NB. I/B = inbound   O/B = outbound   CH = coupon handling

PRINT					
BROCHURE	___	_____	_____	_____	_____
INSERT	___	_____	_____	_____	_____
LEAFLET	___	_____	_____	_____	_____
TAKE-ONE	___	_____	_____	_____	_____
LETTER	___	_____	_____	_____	_____
NEWSLETTER	___	_____	_____	_____	_____
MAGAZINE	___	_____	_____	_____	_____
FOLDER	___	_____	_____	_____	_____
CATALOGUE	___	_____	_____	_____	_____
ENVELOPES	___	_____	_____	_____	_____
HEADED PAPER	___	_____	_____	_____	_____

TOTAL   _____

Notes

This form lists all the elements that will be required in the campaign and should be completed by the campaign manager. The form is critical, as it is the key into the activities and controlling all the detailed elements of the campaign. The term 'element' refers to any deliverable, which may be a physical part of the campaign, such as a letter, or a service, such as deduplication.

In more complex campaigns, the exact tasks being carried out by each supplier may not be known by every supplier. This can cause problems. For example, if promotional material is being prepared by different agencies, and a variety of fulfilment packs will be sent, each prepared by different suppliers, you may be the only one with an overview of all tasks. If something goes wrong, and you are not there to deal with it, problems may be compounded because no-one knows who to warn.

The form will be filled in progressively as the details for the campaign become clear. The campaign manager is likely to be involved in the Y/N decision.

Implementer refers to the member of your staff who is responsible for the particular element.

Supplier co. and supplier contact: In some cases, a supplier will be involved. The name of the supplying company and the contact within that company should also be entered.

Budget is set by the campaign manager. You may not wish to break down costs to this level of detail. In our view, the more detailed your approach, the less vulnerable you will be to overcharging and the better your control of costs will be. However, detail takes time, so you may need to compromise between efficiency and delivery speed.

The deliverables listed on the left hand side are the normal ones for a TAM campaign. Note the specification of different kinds of coupon handling for different media.

Form 5: Initial estimates

CAMPAIGN NAME_____CODE_____

ORIGINATOR_____DATE OF ISSUE_____

	ESTIMATED QUANTITY	ESTIMATED COST (£)
OUTBOUND MAILING	_____	_____
OUTBOUND TAM CALLS	_____	_____
INBOUND COUPON RESPONSE	_____	_____
INBOUND TAM CALLS	_____	_____
FULFILMENT	_____	_____
CONVERSION TO SALE	_____	_____
POSTAGE COSTS		_____
OTHER COSTS		_____
TOTAL COSTS		_____
TOTAL REVENUE		_____

Notes

This section provides a broad quantitative overview of your campaign. To complete these parts of the form, you need to have done your budgeting. This section also informs your team of the key numbers in the campaign, so it serves as early warning of the workload.

The form gives only your first estimates. Good practice suggests that as soon as the need for the campaign is identified, and at the latest after it is given the go ahead, likely costs should be estimated, using your judgement on volume and contact strategies likely to be required. This is input into the final budgeting decision.

For the calculations you need to do to complete this form, use the response rate achieved in the relevant tests or examine similar campaigns (similar products, similar offers) run on similar selections.

The cost elements of the budgeting should be based on anticipated contact and response numbers (including fixed costs). Revenue per response should be gross revenue, as the method of measuring net revenues and contribution may vary. However, if you have an agreed measure, put it in and say so.

Estimated quantity is the volume involved.

Estimated cost is the total cost of each item (not the unit cost).

Outbound mailing is the initial mail pack (cost including design, print and handling by the mailing house, but excluding postage).

Outbound TAM is the telephone contact initiated by TAMs.

Inbound coupon response is the processing of coupons sent in by customers.

Inbound TAM calls is the handling of calls coming in from customers.

Fulfilment: Subsequent mail packs (e.g. catalogues) – cost to include design, print and handling by the mailing house, but excluding postage.

Conversion to sale is the number of actual sales. Costs should include cost of staff time (fully loaded).

Postage costs are the total number of items (mail plus fulfilment) sent, and total postage cost.

Other costs are those not covered above.

Total cost of the above elements should be compared to the planned objective (e.g. sales level, number of contacts).

Form 6: Management and media timing plans

CAMPAIGN NAME_____CODE_____

ORIGINATOR_____DATE OF ISSUE_____

BRIEFING/PLANNING	PLANNED DATE	ACTUAL DATE
Campaign requirement confirmed	_____	_____
Consult TAM management and confirm targeting, timing, offer etc.	_____	_____
Brief mailing/call guide/other agencies	_____	_____
Proposition agreed	_____	_____
Concept agreed	_____	_____
Contact strategy agreed	_____	_____
Media brief produced	_____	_____
Confirm media plan	_____	_____
Receive media details	_____	_____
Issue media details to suppliers	_____	_____
Selections ordered	_____	_____
Lists produced	_____	_____
Go/no go	_____	_____
Check campaign logistics	_____	_____
Brief TAM operations in detail	_____	_____
Campaign live	_____	_____
Campaign ends	_____	_____
Evaluate results	_____	_____

Notes

Forms 6 & 7 between them provide planned and actual dates for each of four sets of tasks, from the overall management set (briefing and planning), to handling of direct marketing media (mail, inbound and outbound TAM work). Media milestones are built in to the briefing and planning set.

The main aim of the forms is to ensure that everyone involved in your campaign knows what they should be doing when. You may not need all the steps, but you are likely to need to diary most of them in. Within each of the four groups of tasks, they are more or less in chronological order, so even if you cannot plan all the dates, you should know that if you get to a particular step and an earlier step has not been completed, something may be wrong.

Fill in the dates actually achieved. Keep all the campaign team up to date with actual achievements, as this will help them plan. If you slip a deadline, it is better to tell everyone about it quickly, rather than waiting until it creates more problems later on.

Form 7: Mail and TAM timing plans

CAMPAIGN NAME_____CODE_____
ORIGINATOR_____DATE OF ISSUE_____

MAIL	PLANNED DATE	ACTUAL DATE
Creative agreed		
Approve pack dummy		
Lists ordered		
Final copy approved		
Mailing/fulfilment house briefed		
Print production schedule issued		
Approve artwork		
Artwork ready for print		
Laser proof approved		
Sign off live pack		
First mailing		
First fulfilment		

INBOUND TELEMARKETING		
Brief call guide agency		
Scripts agreed for testing		
TAM briefing/training		
Selections tested		
Scripts revised after testing		
Call start		

OUTBOUND TELEMARKETING		
Brief call guide agency		
Scripts agreed for testing		
TAM briefing/training		
Selections tested		
Scripts revised after testing		
Call start		

Form 8: List selection brief

CAMPAIGN NAME_____CODE_____

ORIGINATOR_____DATE OF ISSUE_____

EXCLUSIONS

1._____

2._____

3._____

4._____

SPECIAL INSTRUCTIONS_____

SELECTION 1

PRIORITY_____TREATMENT CODE_____ESTIMATED QUANTITY_____

DESCRIPTION_____

CRITERIA_____

_____

_____

_____

_____

_____

TAM AREAS_____

_____

_____

_____

and so on for each selection

INTERNAL LIST SELECTION

List ID_____Decription_____

Selection from list_____

_____

Exclude_____

Database count_____Approved_____

Notes

This form instructs your database team how to identify which TAM customers are going to receive particular treatments. The term 'treatment' refers to the particular version of the campaign, i.e. creative (e.g. letter, call-guide) and medium (mail, TAM, press advertisement) a customer segment will receive as their first contact.

Exclusions are those on your database to be excluded from all treatments in this campaign (e.g. known competitive customers, small businesses).

Special instructions will include any special instructions to the database team concerning how they are to go about selecting customers.

Priority is where there is a possible overlap between selections for different treatments within the campaign. If so, we need to know in which treatment to put customers who belong to more than one group. Thus customers in priorities 1 and 2 would be put into 1).

Treatment code refers to the campaign treatment code.

Estimated quantity is your estimate of the number of people that need to be contacted to achieve the campaign objective. If the number that satisfies the selection criteria is significantly different, then the database team know that they should call you to see whether you want to change their criteria.

Description refers to a simple description of the type of customers being targeted for the treatment (e.g. customers with product A installed).

Criteria refers to specific selection criteria laid down by you to select customers noted in the description (e.g. customers who have bought product A from us in the last five years).

TAM areas refers to which TAM areas customers are to be selected for.

Internal list selection

Your database may be subdivided for marketing purposes into several lists – possibly overlapping. For example, you may have a list of responders to previous promotions, a list of small customers, or a list of known buyers of competitive products. This situation is most likely if your database is relatively new. In this case, selecting whole lists or parts of those lists will be an efficient way of making your selection. This is because the characteristics of these lists are likely to be known. In some cases (e.g. lists of top customers), approval to use them may be required. Such customers should be addressed as a separate selection, as you should be communicating with them in a different way (i.e. different creative).

List ID is the reference number of the list you want to use.

Description refers to the description of the list.

Selection from list is your criteria for selecting from the list.

Exclude refers to any exclusions from the selection.

Database count is your estimate of the number that your criteria will select. This may seem to put the cart before the horse, but if the list characteristics are well known, you should have some idea how many your selection will produce. This will tell the database team that they should contact you if the selection produces a number very different from this. If you have direct access to the system, then this number will be the actual number selected by your criteria.

Form 9: Contact and fulfilment strategy

CAMPAIGN NAME_____CODE_____

ORIGINATOR_____DATE OF ISSUE_____

PRODUCT OFFER LIST

1._____

2._____

3._____

4._____

5._____

6._____

7._____

8._____

CONTACT STRATEGY

STEP ID_____ACTION_____

TARGET SEGMENT_____

PRODUCT OFFERS_____

START DATE_____END DATE_____TIME INTERVAL TO NEXT STEP_____

and so on for each step.

FULFILMENT

ITEM CODE	PACK	REF NO.	STEP ID	NAME AND DESCRIPTION
_____	_____	_____	_____	_____
_____	_____	_____	_____	_____
_____	_____	_____	_____	_____
_____	_____	_____	_____	_____

Please note

This form specifies the contact strategy in detail. It may be changed as you check and revise strategy. Diagrams to be attached, with each action coded

144

Notes

This form summarizes some aspects of your strategy for contacting and responding to TAM customers.

Product offer list is the description of the different product offers which form this campaign.

Step ID: If there are several steps to a campaign (e.g. outbound TAM call, letter, inbound TAM call), it is good practice to give each step an ID. This makes it easier to deal with from a systems point of view.

Action is what is done in the step (e.g. TAM outbound call, mail letter, mail brochure).

Product offer is the offer to be made in this step in this campaign.

Start date is when this step starts to be taken (e.g. for outbound TAM call).

End date is when this step stops. Both start and end date are likely to apply only to the first step, as the dates for other steps will be determined by the speed of customer response. However, there may be an end date placed on last step, to signify the end of the campaign.

Time interval to next step is the time that should be allowed between one step and the next. For example, after a brochure has been sent by the TAM operation, how long should it be before the TAM calls to ask for an order?

Fulfilment specifies which items are in which packs.

Item code is the code number for the item.

Pack refers to the pack it is to go into (e.g. mail responders' pack).

Ref No. is the reference number of the pack.

Step ID is the step in which the pack is sent.

Name and description is the description of the item.

Form 10: Contact strategy diagrams

CAMPAIGN NAME_____CODE_____

ORIGINATOR_____DATE OF ISSUE_____

Segment name

Segment ID
Segment type
Contact step
Media:
  Contact
  Response
Offer type
Pack ID
No. pieces
Pages

Segment name

Segment ID
Segment type
Step name
Media:
  Contact
  Response
Offer type
Pack ID
No. pieces
Pages

Notes

This diagram summarizes how you are going to be identifying and contacting your target customers. In each box, you should complete the following details:

Segment ID is the ID number of the selection – allocated by your system. If you do not have a system for coding selections, you should. Each selection becomes in effect a list you have used, and may want to use again. At each stage of the campaign, different lists will be generated (initial target, responders, non-responders, etc.). Unless you have a system for referring to them, your handling of the database could become cumbersome.

Segment type is a brief description of the segment.

Contact step is the name and ID of the step (e.g. initial contact, follow-up).

Media (contact or response) states what media you are using for the contact and by what media you expect to receive the response.

Offer type says what kind of offer you are making. You should have a system for classifying offers (e.g. price discount, two for one).

Pack ID is the ID of the pack used.

No. pieces is the number of pieces in the pack.

Pages is the number of pages in the pack.

This diagram may look very detailed, but we believe that a good diagram (however large the paper!) provides the clearest way of conveying the structure of your campaign. It also makes sure you leave no loose ends.

Form 11: Selection feedback report

CAMPAIGN NAME_____CODE_____

ORIGINATOR_____DATE OF ISSUE_____

TAM AREA	TREATMENT	QUANTITY PULLED
_____	_____	_____
_____	_____	_____
_____	_____	_____
_____	_____	_____
_____	_____	_____
_____	_____	_____
_____	_____	_____
_____	_____	_____

COMPLETION DATE_____

COMMENTS (e.g. problems in interpreting brief or selecting data)

_____

_____

_____

Notes

After your database team has completed its programming/selection work, you need to be briefed on the results. If you have direct access to the system, this form will not be needed.

Tam area is the TAM operation for which the selection was made.

Treatment is the ID and description of the treatment.

Quantity pulled is the number of customers satisfying the treatment selection criteria.

Completion data is the date on which selection was made. This might be important where the number satisfying the selection criteria was changing quickly.

Comments refers to space for the database team to comment on the brief they received.

Form 12: Outbound TAM calling

CAMPAIGN NAME_____CODE_____

ORIGINATOR_____DATE OF ISSUE_____

TREATMENT ID_____

OBJECTIVES

1._____

2._____

3._____

4._____

PRIME INFORMATION REQUIRED FROM RESPONDENT TO ACHIEVE OBJECTIVES

_____

_____

_____

_____

QUERIES LIKELY TO ARISE DURING CALL

1._____

2._____

3._____

DETAILS TO BE GIVEN TO RESPONDENT (INCLUDING WHAT WILL HAPPEN AFTER CALL)

1._____

2._____

3._____

NON-ROUTINE REPORTING REQUIREMENTS

_____

_____

PLEASE INCLUDE COPIES OF ALL TELEMARKETING SCRIPTS AT DRAFT AND FINAL STAGE

PLEASE INCLUDE CODING DETAILS FOR ANSWERS

Notes

Objectives are those of the call (e.g. to ask for a catalogue order, to commit to a product demonstration, to close an order of a specific value, etc.).

Treatment ID is the ID number of treatment.

Prime information required is what we want to know.

Queries likely to arise during call are the sort of questions the respondent is likely to ask the caller.

Details to be given to respondent are what the customer must be told.

Non-routine reporting requirements are reports other than those normally provided required during and after the campaign.

Fulfilment after call refers to which fulfilment pack/letter is to be sent after the call, and how.

Next steps in contact strategy refers to what the next step the TAM or others (e.g. field sales) should take.

Form 13: Inbound TAM calling

CAMPAIGN NAME_____CODE_____

ORIGINATOR_____DATE OF ISSUE_____

TREATMENT ID_____

PLANNED SOURCE OF RESPONSE_____

OBJECTIVES OF ENQUIRY HANDLING

1._____

2._____

3._____

4._____

PRIME INFORMATION REQUIRED FROM CALLER

_____

_____

_____

_____

QUERIES LIKELY TO ARISE DURING CALL

1._____

2._____

3._____

DETAILS TO BE GIVEN TO CALLER (INCLUDING WHAT WILL HAPPEN AFTER CALL)

1._____

2._____

3._____

NON-ROUTINE REPORTING REQUIREMENTS

_____

_____

PLEASE INCLUDE COPIES OF ALL TELEMARKETING SCRIPTS AT DRAFT AND FINAL STAGE

PLEASE INCLUDE CODING DETAILS FOR ANSWERS

Notes

Treatment ID is the ID number of treatment

Planned source of response is where you specify where the response will be coming from to TAMs (e.g. mailing), and the dates when customers will be exposed to the source.

Objectives of enquiry handling (e.g. to check strength of interest, to commit to a product demonstration, to close an order etc).

Prime information required is what we want to know.

Queries likely to arise during call are the sort of questions the respondent is likely to ask the caller.

Details to be given to caller are what the customer must be told.

Non-routine reporting requirements are those other than normally required during and after the campaign.

Fulfilment after call refers to which fulfilment pack/letter is to be sent after the call, and how

Next steps in contact strategy refers to what the next step the TAM or others (e.g. field sales) should take.

Form 14: Questionnaire summary

CAMPAIGN NAME_____CODE_____

ORIGINATOR_____DATE OF ISSUE_____

ADDITIONAL QUESTIONS FOR CALL GUIDE

1._____

2._____

3._____

4._____

5._____

MAIL QUESTIONNAIRE ID_____

QUESTION DESCRIPTION	ANSWER DESCRIPTION	QUEST. ID NO.	ANS. CODE

Notes

This summarizes the questionnaires to be used in your campaign. As these may be of many different types, this form is placed here as a prompt that the questions to be asked must be set down clearly in order to brief all involved.

Additional questions for call guide: There are many standard questions in guides which need not be covered here (e.g. identifiers). Here are listed the questions special to the campaign.

This form also provides a convenient way of summarizing a mail questionnaire. It will help you brief the house handling data entry for incoming questionnaires. The terms used are as follows:

Mail questionnaire ID is ID of the questionnaire.
Question description is a short description of the question.
Answer description is a short description of the answer.

Question ID is the ID number for the question. Some questions might be asked in several different campaigns. A record of these questions should be asked, and each given ID numbers, so that the data can be collated across campaigns.
Answer code is the code you have assigned to the respective answer.

The process for setting up a questionnaire is as follows:

1   Draft the questions you want to ask.
2   Identify relevant questions already asked in previous campaigns.
3   Determine whether you can use these questions (and/or whether you can use some of the data already gathered).
4   Finalize the questionnaire.
5   Enter the questionnaire details on the form and into your database system. Then send it to the TAM operation or whoever is handling the questionnaire responses (e.g. a fulfilment house).

Form 15: Fulfilment pack summary

CAMPAIGN NAME_____CODE_____

ORIGINATOR_____DATE OF ISSUE_____

PACK CODE_____DESCRIPTION_____

ITEM CODE_____TITLE_____

QUANTITY_____ESTIMATED RESPONSE_____MINIMUM STOCK LEVEL_____

DUE DATE FOR DELIVERY_____

SUPPLIER_____

CONTACT NAME_____TEL NO._____

and so on for each item in pack. Use new form for each pack

Notes

This schedule forms part of the brief to the fulfilment house. It may be expanded when the literature/print process is developed.

Pack code is as specified by you.

Description of pack is, for example, a pack for responders to letter ID No. xxyy.

Item code is the code of each item in pack.

Title is that of each item in pack.

Quantity is the number required for campaign.

Estimated response is the expected number of respondents.

Minimum stock level is the minimum number of item to be held in stock.

Due date for delivery is when stocking point can expect to receive the item.

Supplier is where the item is coming from.

Contact name and telephone No. refers to who and how to contact a supplier of item.

Form 16: Letter summary

CAMPAIGN NAME_____CODE_____

ORIGINATOR_____DATE OF ISSUE_____

PACK CODE_____DESCRIPTION_____

COPY SUPPLIER_____

CONTACT NAME_____TEL NO._____

LASERED _____ PRE-PRINTED _____ DROP-INS _____

TAM SIGNATURE (y/n)_____

LETTERHEAD

TAM_____REGION_____HQ_____PRODUCT GROUP_____OTHER_____

SPECIAL INSTRUCTIONS

_____

_____

Repeat for further letters

Notes

This form ensures that the letter is prepared properly and matched to the right pack.

Pack code is the code of pack in which letter is to be inserted.

Letter description is the description of letter (e.g. letter to respondents requesting more information about product x).

Copy supplier is the company or department responsible for supplying copy.

Contact name and *Tel. No.* refer to the person in that company or department.

Lasered, pre-printed or drop-ins describes how the body of the letter is prepared.

TAM signature is whether a TAM signature is required.

Letterhead: National or regional sales/marketing, customer service, product manager, TAM, etc.

Special instructions refers to any further special instructions.

Form 17: Print production and distribution brief

CAMPAIGN NAME_____CODE_____

ORIGINATOR_____DATE OF ISSUE_____

PACK CODE_____ ORDER QUANTITY_____

DATE OF ORDER_____ OUTBOUND MAILING OR FULFILMENT_____

PRINTER_____DUE DATE OF DELIVERY_____MINIMUM STOCK LEVEL_____

STORE AT_____ COST_____

and so on for each item

Notes

This form briefs staff on print distribution and storage.

Pack code is the code of pack.

Order quantity and date is the quantity in this order and date of this order.

Outbound mailing or fulfilment is the use of this item.

Printer refers to the company printing this item.

Due date of delivery is when item due in stock.

Minimum stock is that to be held at distribution centre.

Store at refers to the location of storage.

Cost refers to cost per item.

Form 18: Sales and service delivery

CAMPAIGN NAME_____CODE_____

ORIGINATOR_____DATE OF ISSUE_____

ORGANIZATION/MANAGER RESPONSIBLE FOR DELIVERY_____

ORGANIZATION/MANAGER RESPONSIBLE FOR INSTALLATION_____

CONTRACT TYPE_____

ORDER PROCESSING INSTRUCTIONS_____

PRICE/PAYMENT TERMS_____

INSTALLATION/DELIVERY INSTRUCTIONS_____

FIELD SALES ACTIONS_____

Notes
This form briefs all those who handle the customer after the sale. The exact content depends very much on your company's particular systems, procedures and products. We have included some examples of what you might want to put on such a form.

Organization/manager responsible for delivery refers to the department responsible for delivery of the product.
Organization/manager responsible for installation refers to the department responsible for installation (if different from the above).
Contract type is the particular type of contract that is to be made out for the product (e.g. lease, sale, guarantee terms, etc.).
Order processing instructions are any special instructions (e.g. the maximum time after the sale is agreed that the order should be processed by).
Price/payment terms is when the customer should pay, and whether there are special price or payment terms.
Installation/delivery instructions are those particular instructions that go with products sold in this campaign.
Field sales actions: If a field sales call is agreed, this refers to what should take place, and how soon after the telephone call.

14

Telemanaging in action

Telemanaging in action will finally be considered with respect to some examples of how the TAM concept can be applied in a variety of businesses and our conclusions about the success factors in TAM. For the examples, we have selected one type of business for analysis of TAM opportunities in detail (the motor dealership), followed by a number of shorter examples, each differing in their customer and product types, and showing the wide range of applications of TAM.

The examples

A large motor dealership

Most large dealerships sell not only one or more ranges of saloon cars, but also light trucks, finance, service, parts, car hire, insurance and possibly fuel. Their customers are likely to include:

- fleet buyers of all sizes (depending on whether their supplier deals with very large fleets directly)
- the private and small business market for executive saloons
- consumer customers for new and used family cars and small saloons.

In some cases, these will be second and third cars in the family
- the rental market – mostly business customers during the week and consumers at weekends
- all customers, for extended warranty, service, accessories and parts
- consumer and small business customers for finance and insurance

The main opportunities for using TAM in this situation would be as follows:

- *Replacement purchasing* – It could establish likely replacement dates (either at time of purchase or by questionnaire during regular servicing) and initiate a structured calling cycle leading up to replacement.
- *New business* – Occasional callers and respondents to advertisements in local or regional media (TV, press and radio) could be assigned a TAM. The TAM could then handle them through to a first (or second) visit to the showroom, and help the salesman conclude the sale. Afterwards a follow-up call could be made, perhaps with the objective of booking the first service visit.
- *Service business* – For existing and new clients, the TAM could ensure that after each service, the next service was booked. If the customer was particularly satisfied, the same service team could be deployed on

165

his car. If there were problems, these could be quickly identified and the customer given an incentive to book again.

- *Customer care* – All customers could be called after they had transacted any business with the company, to check that they were satisfied and identify opportunities for further transactions.
- *Motor insurance* – The company could identify renewal dates and offer insurance which was restricted to the particular make of car sold by the dealership.
- *Rental business* - In some cases, rental business is a distress business (e.g. if the customer's main vehicle is off the road). Where this is for a regular or pre-booked service, the need for a hire vehicle could be identified at the time of booking. In other cases, it would be necessary to use contacts made for other purposes to identify whether the customer ever rents. For private consumers, the economics of rental are likely to rule out prospecting activity dedicated to rental. For commercial customers, particularly ones which are frequent renters, telemanagement would probably pay.

Large insurance companies

In the early 1990s, many companies in this business, whether general or life companies, have been diversifying their product portfolios. Entry into insurance by companies from other finance sectors has increased competitive threats, while the costs of maintaining agencies has led to the examination of alternative, more direct, ways of doing business. In the UK, this has been hastened by new regulatory requirements.

Much of the business in life insurance, pensions and investment products is with high net worth individuals, often small business people. Salespersons or sales agents tend to 'skim' the market, concentrating only on those customers with high investment needs and willingness to commit their funds to longer term investments. TAM could be used to ensure in-depth penetration of all customers, rather than just the high net worth ones, enabling a company to develop the value of the whole market.

The basic business of insurance selling – inbound call handling, quotation giving, conclusion of the deal, and renewal management – could certainly be handled by a dedicated TAM-type operation. However, with most customers holding single policies from any one company, true account management would not pay. However, TAM might be used for cross-selling into other product categories. Once a customer has several policies, account managing them would become feasible. TAM could be particularly effective in larger accounts, where there might be group schemes (health, pension, etc.).

Retail banks

Most banks currently transact most of their business through a network of branches. However, many are now considering new ways of managing two kinds of customers:

- high net worth individuals
- small and medium businesses

Many banks already have facilities for remote handling of simple transactions, using either an ordinary telephone or a terminal attached to the telephone line. More complex facilities are available to larger commmercial customers. As these facilities are extended to a broader range of customers, TAM could be used for full account management, including account query, complicated transactions, instructions and cross-selling of savings and loan products. As banks enter into investment and insurance products, TAM could be used for cross-selling.

Computer companies

Most computer companies sell equipment, supplies and services. Their customers range from the largest multinational corporation to the smallest business and consumers. Most now have a basic telemarketing and catalogue operation. TAM is ideal for dealing with medium and small-potential customers, but also for non-centralized buyers in larger organizations, as well as centralized buying of suppliers, services and peripherals. TAM can handle inbound enquiries off the catalogue, full order taking and outbound campaigns. TAM could also be used to support the field sales force, which concentrates on selling major equipment and complex services.

Consumer mail-order catalogue companies

Most mail-order catalogue companies sell almost entirely by post to consumers. Most have opened inbound telemarketing operations, which provide quicker service and enable the consumer to check whether the required items are in stock. However, higher value customers would certainly benefit from the TAM approach. This would enable companies to:

- improve service to their accounts
- speed up implementation of special promotions (e.g. by telephoning special offers through)
- ensure quicker feedback to company on product lines
- offer a personalized service to high spenders, to tailor packages and

select suitable new products, based on an understanding of the individual customer's needs – an approach already used extensively in the USA.

Direct-selling holiday companies

Amongst the direct-selling holiday companies, a number are emerging which concentrate on more up-market holidays, typically to very high class resorts or hotels, or to remote locations. Many of their customers typically take three to four holidays a year at values per head four to five times the national average, often travelling in pairs. Such companies may start to attract corporate customers, perhaps for sales incentive trips.

Such companies could use TAM to:

- market existing products
- cross-sell between categories of holiday
- achieve early estimates of take up of new products through research
- improve customer care
- validate quality by post-holiday calls

Leisure complex

As the proportion of income spent on leisure increases, and as consumers start to develop more and more varied leisure pursuits, many leisure complexes are being set up to meet the demand for mental and physical recreation. Currently, they obtain most of their business either through close contact with those who are members of the club, or through advertisements in local and regional media. If such a complex wanted to increase its business through addition of appropriate new products and prospecting for more up-market customers, it could use TAM for:

- screening of membership applications arising from enquiries from leaflets and local press and managing the conversion of resulting prospects
- cross-selling of events
- research for new products
- customer care

Marketing service companies

Most marketing services companies seek to expand their client base and to penetrate more deeply into existing clients. In larger companies, there may be some decentralized buying of marketing services. However, to all but the largest such companies, the cost of a calling account management team can be high. This may be exacerbated because many clients in the marketing world seem to be difficult to contact!

TAM could perhaps be used to handle some client-contact work and to produce some new business within existing accounts. For the latter, the key need is to get properly qualified appointments, and then follow up by identifying likely timing and nature of request for quote.

Success factors

What are the main points to learn from TAM? They are these:

- If you commit yourself to TAM, allow enough time to implement it. If your company is large, phase the introduction of TAM to allow yourself to learn from each step. Pilot

the concept if at all possible.
- Plan it properly. TAM requires managing much detail which should not be left to the last minute. Plan in detail from the beginning. Use project management disciplines.
- Recruit and train your TAMs and their support staff carefully. Do not transfer other staff into the operation without being absolutely sure that they fit the profile. When you are certain that you have staffed the TAM operation properly, train all TAM staff, especially in account management, telephone handling of customers and in products.
- If you have a main customer database, integrate the TAM operation with your company's database marketing approach. Make this integration work for systems, marketing planning and media usage.
- Communicate what you are planning and what you are doing, as early as possible. Pay particular attention to staff who may feel threatened. Try to involve them in your work.
- Use established systems and software wherever possible. Do not be tempted to use leading edge technology. TAM does not require the most advanced systems. It requires reliable systems which are easy to use.
- In large companies, plan a long-term campaign of change. Try to time it to coincide with a general move in the direction of database marketing. Do not expose TAM by making it stand alone. Position TAM carefully as an account management method, and distance it from teleselling.

If you do all these, and if your market analysis is correct, then TAM should work for you.

Index